Come What May

Also by Lucy Easthope

When The Dust Settles: Stories of Love,
Loss and Hope from an Expert in Disaster

COME WHAT MAY

Life-Changing Lessons for Coping with Crisis

LUCY EASTHOPE

hodder
press

First published in Great Britain in 2025 by Hodder Press
An imprint of Hodder & Stoughton Limited
An Hachette UK company

The authorised representative in the EEA is Hachette Ireland, 8 Castlecourt Centre, Dublin 15, D15 XTP3, Ireland (email: info@hbgi.ie)

2

Copyright © Lucy Easthope 2025

The right of Lucy Easthope to be identified as the Author of the Work has been asserted by her in accordance with the Copyright, Designs and Patents Act 1988.

All rights reserved. No part of this publication may be reproduced, stored in a retrieval system, or transmitted, in any form or by any means without the prior written permission of the publisher, nor be otherwise circulated in any form of binding or cover other than that in which it is published and without a similar condition being imposed on the subsequent purchaser.

A CIP catalogue record for this title is available from the British Library

Graph on page 21 by Clare Payne.

Hardback ISBN 9781399736213
ebook ISBN 9781399736220

Typeset in Plantin Light by Hewer Text UK Ltd, Edinburgh
Printed and bound in Great Britain by Clays Ltd, Elcograf S.p.A.

Hodder & Stoughton policy is to use papers that are natural, renewable and recyclable products and made from wood grown in sustainable forests. The logging and manufacturing processes are expected to conform to the environmental regulations of the country of origin.

Hodder Press
Hodder & Stoughton Limited
Carmelite House
50 Victoria Embankment
London EC4Y 0DZ

www.hodderpress.co.uk

This book is dedicated to all those that we lost in these times and to those that miss them every day.

Contents

Introduction	1
Lesson One: Walking the Path	15
Lesson Two: Taking Stock	41
Lesson Three: After the Honeymoon	75
Lesson Four: Needful Things	95
Lesson Five: Bad Help	121
Lesson Six: Hopium	139
Lesson Seven: Holding Two Truths	163
Lesson Eight: Survivance	189
Lesson Nine: Painting Your Kintsugi	207
Lesson Ten: By Hammer and Hand	229
End Note: Whatever Next	253
Acknowledgements	259
Further Reading	263
Notes	267
Index	273

Introduction

We all see moments of crisis in our lives, whether it's something personal that happens to us and our families, or to our community, or something that we experience more at a distance, as part of being in the world. The last few years, living inside a pandemic, means that we are all disaster survivors now. We all know loss and grief of various kinds. We will see failure and disappointment and heartbreak. We may say goodbye to a beloved pet, wait for a consultant to give a life-changing diagnosis, separate our lives from a partner. There will be times that feel hard and relentless, with no moment to breathe out.

My own experience of disaster is different to most other people's because of the job I do. I am an emergency planner. I have worked on almost every disaster involving British citizens in some capacity and given advice on others overseas for years. Emergency planners work before the disaster, during the disaster and after the disaster. We make big, long lists of all the things that can go wrong in the world and then work out what to do about them. We think about the winter in the spring. You will find me alongside those who prepare us for emergencies and those who try to prevent them. I am not a first responder; the calls to me come in later. My own particular speciality is in the aftermath, the clean-up and, hopefully, the rebuild. I am the last responder.

In my work, I have come to know what survival means in the context of some of the world's biggest tragedies. The capsized ferries. The wreckage of airliners within collapsed buildings. I have seen a single day's death toll counted in hundreds of thousands. I have seen two million personal effects belonging to victims gathered in a year-long operation. I have seen people pick themselves up after their home has literally washed away.

This is a book about what a life in disaster has taught me about how we go on, during and after terrible times. It's about the lessons that have revealed themselves to me through witnessing the weeks and months after disaster over and over again. And about the lessons that have come home with me and mended me when I needed them.

It is also a responsive book, born out of listening to people from all around the world who are trying to make sense of the challenging times we are living through. People are more interested in what comes next than I have ever known. As the climate changes and tensions between countries ignite, people are worried and looking for new ways to navigate this territory. But those pathways have always been there, and it is often in the stories of past disasters that they become clearer.

Introduction

The preparation and planning work my colleagues and I do usually goes unheeded by the world outside my small professional community. You don't get to see all the near misses we prevent or the times that we do meet everyone's needs in a crisis. These things don't make the news. So the times that we learn and teach good, helpful things, things that can make the difference, get lost. When we do have profound impact on a situation, the work does not get seen. It's time to hear about the wins as well.

This book comes from my desire to share the good, helpful things I have learned with people who are trying to navigate some of the hardest things in human experience, the everyday personal disasters, and who might feel lost and in need of guidance. Perhaps you have found this book because you have been trying to find a path through your own cataclysm. And you are getting through. Though you probably are not giving yourself nearly enough credit.

I want to share with you the tools and lessons that I have seen have a real impact in getting an individual or a community through a disastrous event. So each chapter deals with my experiences from working in disasters and distils a truth that can help us not just survive but grow and learn from our difficult experiences. Lessons about how to triage your life to avoid feeling overwhelmed, letting go of failures and disappointments, making sure you compartmentalise the pain to give yourself a break from it, planning for the slump that so often follows the initial trauma, helping others experiencing a disaster and what good help looks like.

Some of what I have been taught in my career has surprised and challenged me, but has also ultimately comforted me, and I think it will be useful to you too. I have seen green shoots of new beginnings and moments of the purest of joys. I have seen over and over again how the pressure of crisis gives a visual acuity that focuses the mind like nothing else. My real hope is that these stories and the lessons I have learned from them might change your life.

The long, difficult years of the coronavirus pandemic and the global lockdowns showed that disasters don't just happen to other people. Every one of us experienced the pandemic differently and with different types of loss. But all of our lives were bent out of their normal shapes by something over which we had no control.

In early 2020, at the start of the Covid pandemic, while I was still coughing incessantly from my own serious encounter with the infection, the calls started to come in confirming that the thing we had feared was here. A pandemic had been at the top of the lists we create to identify and prioritise risks in the UK. It was time to get very ready.

At first, people did not want to think about it in terms of a disaster. I would watch them wince at the D word when I used it in the early stages of the pandemic. I still see some resistance now – a closing of faces and an attempt to bat the toll away. But the pandemic gets to take its place as a world-changing catastrophic event. We have all been forced to recognise that serious things happen that are well out of our hands. We have faced our mortality and our fears. The helplessness, the sudden loss of 'normal' life and routines, the railing against the arbitrary nature of fate, the feeling of powerlessness and often anger against authority. There are the obvious losses for some, like bereavement or loss of health, and then other losses that you can't quite put a finger on – the grief for the 'before', perhaps.

For a time, we were all briefly united by one specific disaster and it is something that will always be part of our experience. We are now in the 'after' and all of us will have learned things about ourselves, and about life and death, from those years. Life will continue to bring all sorts of hardships, from the large scale to the small scale. Some of these things will be out of our control. They will seem to be without reason or fairness. But what is in our control is how prepared we are for them – for both the road ahead and the aftermath – so we can survive with as much of ourselves whole as possible. We can be forever changed but still here.

After experiencing something as world-altering as a global pandemic, when we were all taught to be afraid, it's hard not to feel on edge, more anxious, seeing danger and possible disaster round every corner. But is the world actually any more dangerous than it ever was? It's a difficult question to answer. The world can seem much more threatening, partly because of how we consume news about it, how increased access to information forces us to be more aware of the risks. One of my coping strategies for dealing with this head on is to read *a lot* and to constantly vary the sources of the information I consume. Advances in medicine mean that disease is much less likely to kill us. But advances in warfare mean it is easier to take out whole populations than ever before. Geopolitical tensions are high. And then there is the changing climate. There is certainly a constant stream of world events to keep me busy. And there is newer and more urgent need to understand survival and recovery than we have seen for decades.

The way that we are being exposed to a world in crisis is changing and that can leave us terrified and exhausted. In my work, we are using the word 'permacrisis' a lot – a constant sense of hurtling from one major event to the next without fallow periods or the time to draw breath. The imagery that accompanies permacrisis is immediate, unedited and unfiltered. As people see more and more images and videos posted of conflicts around the world (from Sudan, Gaza, Ukraine and ninety other wars currently raging), they exclaim that now war is different, doing new harms. Sometimes they ask me how it's possible to cope when you have seen the human form torn into shreds. But to me, these photos and videos are the same as the ones I had seen many times before. War has looked like that for centuries. In the past, though, prior to widespread access to social media, the videos were captured, yes, but not broadcast by news corporations. Before, they were kept by the military and the police to be played on big screens at the training events that I have spent my career attending. Now people are exposed via their social media to things that only responders, the military and the people caught up in the events used to see. The imagery darts into their eyeline when they least expect it. Bad news, delivered breathlessly, sells. But have the risks actually gone up? That question is complicated, even for someone like me who has made risk their job. Risk is not spread equally, but for some communities life is as dangerous as at any other time in history.

Being an emergency planner means, naturally, that I am a planner. I believe in the merits of having a plan and then making sure it has some flex in it. I loathe the adage that 'plans don't survive contact with the enemy', meaning they don't survive when tested or when they confront reality. Good plans do. And my hope is that this book will help you form a plan for yourself, not so you can live in a permanently anxious state expecting danger round every corner, but so that you have a plan if you should ever need it. As Maya Angelou said: 'Hoping for the best, prepared for the worst.'

I have learned from the best – from police officers, forensic scientists, paramedics, funeral directors and, of course, other emergency planners. But the person who gave me the earliest and best lessons was my dad. Bob Payne was a walking audio book of scouse parables and stories of links to past disasters, big and very, very small. He had administered CPR, both successfully and not. He had used his immense strength to lift wreckage. As a teacher, he had held back young lads as they tried to head out to the Toxteth riots of 1981 armed with tools they had stripped from his school carpentry workshop. I don't think I ever saw him pass up a chance to help and help well. My mum is horrified that some of my and my sister's most vibrant early childhood memories are of him stopping at accident scenes. He went in as others were leaving. I saw my very first dead man, a pedestrian hit by a car, as my dad directed the traffic around him so that a now futile ambulance could pull up at the kerb. Then, when he was no longer needed, he would slip away.

I was born being able to see the tiger in the undergrowth. Even the one that was really hidden, the one that some people might walk past or ignore or mistake for a rug. I have always sensed what is coming next in a sequence of harms as a caustic tingling, with a certainty and an urgency that made me a terrible employee. I am earnest and well-meaning but also interfering and dogged. As a child, I would pull on shirt cuffs until an adult heard my note of caution and did something meaningful about it. My mum and dad would tell a story of how, when I was seven years old, I sat them down and explained patiently why taking the stabilisers off my bike was a really bad idea. Stabilisers, I argued, were essential. For stabilisation. I painted a detailed picture of a horrific fall, an unsurvivable head injury and their own guilt. They relented, and my bike retained its two big wheels and two small wheels. I failed my cycling proficiency test on that very bike (it turns out that the examiners did insist on just two wheels). The thing is, I don't remember being afraid, just certain. I am neither a fearful person nor a catastrophist. I have just always seen risk slightly differently and wanted to explore what came after its realisation. To see risk and work out what to do with it seems to be how I am configured, and this capacity has formed the basis of my professional life.

As I began to speak publicly about my experiences as an emergency planner, I received more and more questions on my own personal thoughts about risk. It became clear that people thought that doing this job, creating those long lists of all the things that could go wrong, would make me much more afraid. That I would not be able to live with the rattling of fate. In fact, one of my greatest life lessons is the opposite. I learned it first from my dad: to live alongside the tigers. It takes some work but that is the balance we all have to find: to embrace what comes next and not be fearful.

As emergency planners, our profession probably serves to hold a lot of our anxiety in check because we are allowed to talk openly about fears and worries and then call it a job. I have come to realise that's one of the best things about it. To worry out loud but also talk about the mitigations and the sources of hope is what everyone needs.

Almost four decades after I campaigned for my stabilisers to stay on, I watch my own daughter navigate a showjumping course on half a ton of horse. Safety kit in place but no stabilisers. In my role as a mother, I have to calibrate exactly the balance between the importance of saying aloud what might happen and the importance of both of my daughters' chances to be free. I have to decide which bits of my life lessons to pass on and which bits should be left out.

Every few months, I sit down with Bex, a senior emergency planner based in the West Midlands of the UK. We meet for pancakes and syrup and fruit smoothies. The serving staff have learned to leave us alone as we debrief. As part of our conversation, we do something that I have noticed a lot of emergency planners delight in: we range through a great breadth of subjects at lightning speed and pepper our talk with shared acronyms. We discuss bridge collapses and a near-miss with unexploded ordnance and our children's new school years and bird flu. We bring our planner lives into our home lives and tease each other about the way we approach school calendars (with military precision and a weather eye for trouble ahead).

We love planning and we concur that for us, personally, it helps. We also help others by planning. The last time I saw Bex, we talked about how our jobs allow us to do something very healing. If other people were to think so much about planning for the worst, they would be considered obsessive or anxious, but we view it as perfectly normal and sensible. We clink our fruity drinks together in a toast to disaster thinking, to living a life that allows us to consider possible scenarios that often are headed off but sometimes aren't. Because in thinking about them, readying for them, we unleash strengths we never knew we had.

My dad, the most important influence on my life, died suddenly at 11.59pm on 23 April 2023. The birds were singing far too loudly as the sun came up the next morning. My mum and I would have cheerfully shot every single one of them. The two men from the family firm of funeral directors, whose children played with my children, gently wrestled a trolley down my mum's stone steps. I looked for the name of the manufacturer imprinted on the trolley's leg and wryly smiled when I found it. It was a make I knew well. It was strong and reliable and up to the task in hand.

My work had taught me so much about what to do that night – practical things and things that help us to cope. I was grateful that I remembered them. They were things that would lead four paramedics to remark that I had coped well and made good choices in the darkest of nights. But my learning was about to start all over again. It was time to put everything I had ever been taught amongst the chaos into practice, as I navigated my route through this very personal disaster.

In the days that followed Dad's death, dishes piled up in the kitchen, untouched cups of tea went cold and filmy, and the gifted lasagnes arrived. My bookcases groan with grief memoirs and grief survival guides, and many of them detail the lasagne phase. When people try to help with a gift of wholesome food, recreating a rite that is centuries old.

It was these lasagnes, meat and vegetarian, that made me face up to the fact that this crisis was real, and close, and that in order to survive it, I would need my life lessons more than ever. The next months/years/forever were going to be spent testing my life's work from the inside, treading the path of recovery. I had always had a great passion for my work, but suddenly I felt a profound personal gratitude for the insights it had given me. I knew that, at every stage, I would be placing my feet inside footprints left by others. Walking a path. As other people's cookware piled up in the kitchen, I had never before felt such profound gratitude for a life of disaster.

For years, I have watched how people and communities can be stricken and then painfully edge towards what comes next: the work, the pitfalls and the fragile joy woven through the aftermath. In this book, I distil what these sacred places have taught me, examining the questions that are often posed to me as a responder and recoverer after tragedy, including the questions I have found hardest to answer.

The word 'disaster' is formed from the Latin *dis* and *astro*, meaning bad stars. It refers to an ancient belief that when the stars are in a certain position, unfortunate events are going to occur. Big and small.

If we are all disaster survivors now, then we urgently need to talk openly about how to survive now. And so this book is for everyone and for all sorts of life events. Anything that challenges us. Anything that feels like a loss. I take the broadest possible view of what 'a disaster' can be for someone. Some of the events I will refer to are some of the biggest, most totemic disasters in our history, but there are lessons within them for all of us.

We talk about 'lessons' a lot in emergency planning and I often worry that the word has lost any meaning or potency. After large-scale catastrophes, people want the lesson learning to be correspondingly grand and scaffolded. To be held in fine buildings and given the title of 'inquiry'. But what I have come to understand is that the real learning is done by the campfire, in the hospital waiting room, the pulpit, the mosque or in the pancake place. That is where the greatest stories are told, packaged carefully to ensure that the light and the grit stay in there. I have been asked often about the events I remember the best or the ones that changed me the most, but the truth is I remember them all – they have taken a place in my soul.

When I first started out, my mentors and more experienced colleagues would tell their veteran stories to us newbies, and we would sit and listen with awe and respect. This had led to disasters themselves as being described as 'heuristics' – a tool that aids discovery and improvement. There is a comfort that comes from walking in well-trodden footprints instead of trying to stumble in the darkness. No matter how unique a set of events may feel when you are caught up in them, other people have been there before you. They found a way. At the end of each time that the stars misaligned, there was a set of new reflections and new chances to learn.

I carry with me one particular story from a colleague whose role in response to a bombing was to find and recover the broken bodies in an office block. As they dug down through the rubble, they made a discovery that was simultaneously ordinary and also everything. One deceased woman was found with her 'walking to work' trainer on one foot and her shiny black 'woman at work' court shoe on the other foot. The seismic force had interrupted life *mid shoe change.*

What we can take from this is that life changes that quickly. Every day, I learn about new interrupted goodbyes and days that panned out like nobody intended. They don't depress me or drag me down. I often wonder if the same parts of my brain that are so attuned to when times go wrong are also the parts of the brain that allow me to relish an exquisite dessert or love with such intensity. They allow me to see uncertainty as a motivator.

The question I am asked the most is how do you live alongside this uncertainty? This knowledge of chaos that lurks behind the door. How do you live knowing there are absolutely no guarantees? And so that is what this book sets out to answer, for all of us who are surviving and living life in the *after.*

Lesson One
Walking the Path

Things can go from nothing to something in a moment. Or so it seems. On the morning of 22 September 1934, the men of the Gresford mine would have woken up as they had a hundred times before. Some must have had their fears and their doubts before this day, which they had probably taken home to their wives. Muttered darkly about the bosses who were pressing them to work harder and make more profit as they lay next to their partner, one arm across her belly, feet entangled, watching the sun rise. She would likely have swallowed her own thoughts down, knowing how unhelpful it would be to share them. Made sure he had his lunch tin packed and a home to come back to. Every shift, he would have to travel down one of the longest mine shafts ever built in this country. But this was the day that would break the chain of identical mornings. These men and women were about to be lifted off their familiar paths and into a new landscape that would take decades to repair.

One type of disaster that has been replicated in almost every continent of the world is an explosion or a collapse in a mine. Mining is still one of the riskiest jobs you can do. One of the deadliest mine disasters in UK history occurred in a small place called Gresford, in Wrexham, North Wales. On Saturday 22 September 1934, the news of a series of terrible explosions and a raging fire was brought to the nearby village by a naked man. His clothes had been burned off and his first action, bloody and burned, was to run home.

Two-hundred-and-sixty-two men and boys died in the initial explosion, three men died in the rescue operation, and the two-hundredth-and-sixty-sixth man died when he was hit by debris on day three of the response. A seal had blown off the pit head while frantic efforts to get to the trapped and dying men were made.

In the days leading up to 22 September, there had been all the signs of impending doom, but the men were conditioned then, as we are now, to shrug them off. In the two years prior to the disaster, corners had been cut. The role of mine agent, the technically experienced engineer who could stand up to the owners with his expertise, had been replaced in name only by a company secretary with none of those skills. His deputy, in charge of safety, was distracted, something he admitted at the later public inquiry. The mine was known for being dry and extremely gassy, and therefore at risk of something called fire damp, which made explosions much more likely. The mine was hot to work in at the best of times but in those days before, the talk will have been that it was hotter than normal. One pit manager had started to be particularly vocal about safety issues at this time, the records show, but the miners were being pressured to work harder than ever.

The explosion occurred in the early hours of the morning, when 480 men were at work. Maybe some died instantly, but we know that for some time, many others did not realise there was an explosion or fire or poisonous gas because they carried on working in their section. The little canaries in their cages, carried in by the first rescue teams, started to die as soon as they were inside. The few men who escaped from other parts of the mine talked of a gust of wind that scattered dust over their food tins. This was enough to tell them something was wrong and they ran along an escape road, taking it in turns to lead because the person at the front was hit hardest by the poisonous gas.

Explosions continued into the week and several men must have been alive for many hours. In just a moment, new, terrible stars for this place had taken up their places. It would take a long time for them to realign.

Eighty-five years later, Ryan Reynolds and Rob McElhenney, two Hollywood actors, bought one of the world's oldest football clubs, Wrexham AFC. It was a team that was really struggling in a town that was also really struggling. Their experiences of ownership are captured in a Disney documentary series, *Welcome to Wrexham*, charting both their highs and lows as club owners but also their relationship with the town.[1] As each series develops, the link between the town's fates and the disaster still within it are occasionally explored.

I actually know this part of the world well. My Nanny Pat and Grandad Reg, my mum's parents, lived there. As children, my sister Clare and I would 'holiday' thirty miles up the road in their bungalow while Mum and Dad renovated a house in Birkenhead. My grandmother was an internationally acclaimed flower arranging demonstrator and judge, so we earned our keep by sorting out her kit ready for the next series of events. There was a perpetual supply of gold spray paint and taffeta.

If we were taken to Wrexham to buy sweets or some Lego, we would avoid Saturdays and Wednesdays so as not to get caught up in the footballing crowds around the Racecourse ground. But even on those days, I always thought it quite a sad, grey place. I would lobby to travel further to Chester instead, which had better ice cream shops. Still, I noticed the articles in the *Wrexham Leader*, the local newspaper, each year about the commemoration service or the death of another ageing survivor. As my interest grew, my grandparents took me to see the colliery wheel at a place called Pant, but they skirted around the edges of the story. The remains of over 250 of the husbands and fathers killed still lie in the mine today. It was a source of great sadness to the remaining relatives that many of the bodies were not recovered out of the ground. It felt like people did not care enough. 'Why couldn't we have Dad out?' asks a woman, now nearly 100, to the American documentary makers of *Welcome to Wrexham*.

As I was watching the first episodes of the documentary series, I enjoyed the football, the American owners' attempts to learn Welsh, their grapplings with Welsh planning laws. But I realised that I was also watching for something else.

I was watching for the recovery graph.

The disaster recovery graph

One of the most frequent statements I hear from those caught up in any kind of destabilising event is that it was an 'unprecedented' happening. There is a tendency towards a strong belief that this terrible thing is the first that has harmed quite like this. And yet, wherever in the world the disaster happens, some aspects of what immediately follows are eerily and wearily familiar. That can be true of many life events, just as it is of catastrophe. Widowhood, redundancy, fall from a ladder, pregnancy loss are at the same time individually specific and collectively the same. They seem to all sweep us up from the road we were walking along and fling us down into a new terrifying landscape. One with no placemarkers, no way to see our course.

But that is an illusion. In fact, there is a path in front of us. One full of challenges we never expected to meet, but a path nonetheless. When it comes to large-scale tragedy, researchers and disaster responders have attempted to write this path down.

(Responders is my shorthand for the collective of people who go in to help straight after disaster. Broadly, I'm thinking of the emergency services, even the army, sometimes charities. Though actually, there may be significant blurring between the groups. We often fall into multiple categories. A fire chief may also be a resident of the worried street. A surgeon may suddenly become a patient of their own specialist disease.)

Books and whole disaster studies conferences are dedicated to exploring when disaster starts, and if it ever ends. By the 1970s, American scholars had begun to analyse the course of world-changing events and debate whether it could in fact be dissected into distinct phases. Those debates continue to this day. Many of them were sparked by a growing recognition that the plane falling from the sky or the tornado whipping through the town may last just a few minutes, but the human consequences of these events lasted far longer. Sometimes they seemed to get harder as time went on. As is the academic way, other scholars joined the debate and contended that the phases overlap and wax and wane. These phases were then drawn into training documents and slides to help responders take a more longitudinal approach to the events unfolding in front of them. These discussions also attempted to make sense of a human need in the aftermath to see things getting better. To codify and frame and describe a 'recovery phase' that would ultimately lead to reconstruction and renewal. The movie ending.

One result of all of this study is the 'disaster recovery graph', which maps the typical emotional highs and lows on the y axis against time passing on the x axis, to give emergency recoverers an imperfect shorthand for the stages that together form disaster aftermath. If you have never heard of this then the shape of it may be surprising.

Soon after the event, there is an eye-catching upward slope, representing an improvement in feelings, perhaps even a type of euphoria, followed by a crash, more deep pits and then, hopefully, and only with favourable winds, a gentle yet stuttering incline. This can be quite a confronting truth and different from what we expect.

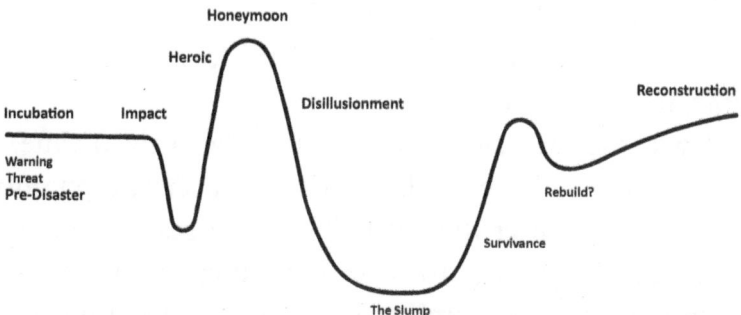

The Disaster Recovery Graph[2]

Versions of this diagram have been developed over seventy years to help planners prepare for the peaks, and mainly troughs, after disaster. I have learned that it works much closer to home too. I have referred to it in all sorts of situations. It's a surprising truth that somehow is useful in terms of how we all can think about the most difficult times in our lives.

As an emergency planner, I have found that I am most helpful in the aftermath of disaster, rather than its emergency response, although delivering training for emergency response in advance is something that will always be important to me. Often, I am asked to deliver a workshop to groups who will be involved – for example, police or local government – in the event of something serious happening to the community, in which I carefully frame some potential fears as things to ready for. Sometimes, I am called on to speak to those same groups again, though now in tumult, in the first few days after an event has occurred. We talk about the luggage-strewn scene or where to build the mortuary. Or how to care for the flowers being left at three main locations. (You start by taking the cellophane which gets in the way of the composting you will need to do in a few days' time, in case you were wondering.)

I will then usually speak to them for a third time. I don't start to talk about the disaster recovery graph until several weeks after the event. The local responders will be gathered together to meet me either online or in a town hall council chamber or swiftly procured meeting room at a cheap hotel. We jostle for coffee and biscuits in a room next door to a speed awareness course.

People hurry in, late, clutching phones, and with eyes that bore into me that this use of their precious time better be bloody worth it. They are exhausted and bone-weary and desperately want someone to tell them that things will get better. Each one has likely worked to well past midnight on the emergency. Just weeks into the worst time their community has seen in recent memory and they have been pulled away from their responsibilities to come to *this*, they are thinking.

Many people fight me on the recovery graph when first shown it in these situations, for reasons I will explain.

So why would I use something that people recoil from? It is because overcoming the initial resistance has always proved worth it.

As with emergency plans themselves – just flimsy A4 pieces of paper, on first glance – the graph does not seem to be revelatory or life changing. But people coming to understand the universality of it has provoked some of the most powerful moments in the meetings I have led following a disaster. It is the most important tool that I have, and I introduce it to both responders and to communities. The graph travels, it talks, and it does a lot more than people expect.

I have learned, therefore, to introduce the graph (see page 21) with great caution. Its revelation can feel theatrical, even vaguely spiritual. It is just a wiggly line on a piece of paper, or on a screen, but it is also so much more than that. I try to show it on a big screen but the IT often fails me and I have been known to pass round my laptop like a congregation plate so that people can see it. It has to be seen.

Intuition

It often surprises people that the disaster recovery graph actually starts before the disaster. The initial part of the line represents 'the pre-event' – the circumstances that may lead up to, cause or influence the conditions of the disaster. Just like in Gresford, where the men's worries about the mine and its management were rumbling under their own surfaces for months and years.

In all aspects of life, there may be an incubation phase, and this can be where our lost art of intuiting becomes relevant, as we start to feel unnerved or begin to pick up hidden cues. We see that corners have been cut. There's a string of near misses. Someone we love hasn't seemed themselves for a while.

I have come to particularly loathe this phase in my work. Cassandras like me may urge and irritate when we see or sense something on the horizon, but all we can really do is wait. As an emergency planner, the likelihood that something is going to happen rattles around in your belly for months and maybe years.

How to understand this stage is one of the most common things I am asked about in my work. *We know, don't we?* people mutter at me. *We knew before.* Maybe they too have felt the tingling, the itch that this train might be halted on the line, that the chap over there is a wrong 'un and wants what is in our bag. That the weather forecasters have got this prediction wrong, that this is the big storm. Or at home, the changing pallor of a loved one, the puffy face that indicates a heart attack is maybe on the cards. At one talk I gave recently, a woman in a bright yellow dress hummed the hit song 'We Don't Talk about Bruno' at me, from the Disney movie *Encanto*. The one about the man with the premonitions who is shunned. 'How do we listen to our Brunos?' she whispered into my ear. I know that this can make me tricky to live with as I berate the kids for carrying too big a load down the staircase (I am always intrigued by the mundane domesticity of many household incidents and the high accident rate linked to items like slippers).

I still don't know entirely what to do with this stage and all emergency planners carry a burden of not being heard several times in their own career. I also don't want anyone to beat themselves up for not doing anything beforehand. Clinicians still don't value intuition or instinct when diagnosing illness and parents of sick children often feel particularly dismissed by the medical profession. In 2023 England and Wales passed new legislation to give parents more rights to a second opinion in such situations. It has given me hope to see better training in areas like medicine for how to listen to the patient's voice when they say in the days or weeks before that something is wrong. Social media has also helped people to find their voice and hone their advocacy.

The moment of impact

Then, with a bang, there is *the moment* itself. The moment when the canaries start to die and the gas inside the mine ignites. On the recovery graph, this is often indicated with a rudimentary orange explosion emoji – even if there wasn't an actual one – to represent one world ending and another beginning. The moment where all the previous life is halted. Dividing time into the life before and the life after.

In our own lives, these explosions can take many forms – loss of a job, loss of health or home, loss of a loved one. My A-level psychology teacher first introduced me to the

Holmes and Rahe scale of stressful life events, an American-designed inventory of forty-three fundamentally important life events, defined as occurrences that are likely to bring about readjustment-requiring changes in people's usual activities. Based on research that was begun in 1967, it places 'death of spouse' firmly at the top,[3] followed by divorce and marital separation. Jail terms, retirement, deaths of other family members and pregnancy also made the top ten. I remember finding it overly simplistic when I first heard about it, disliking the codifying of people's sorrow. But now I see that it's a classic emergency planner's list. An attempt to try to impose order on the messiness of human life.

Euphoria

The next phase, immediately after the event – whether it's a national disaster or a personal loss – is, perhaps surprisingly, a brief upward slope. When 'the thing' happens, there is often an outpouring of support for the person, the people or the place. The term often used for this is 'the honeymoon phase'. Which seems so incongruous and so wrong a word. But there is a reason for this. As news spreads of a tragedy, the response is often a lot of rushed love. People are moved, wanting to help and support. Hugs, compassion, attention can cause a flood of oxytocin and even a brief euphoria.

I know from various eyewitness accounts captured in books and archives that Gresford experienced a brief 'honeymoon', when people around the world flooded it with attention. A fund was established for widows and dependants, of which there were hundreds, and donations arrived from all over the country. The records show that the people of Aberdeen, Scotland, sent boxes of kippers, enough for each family. A telegram of 'fraternal condolence' arrived from Moscow on behalf of the 700,000 coal miners of Russia.[4]

This ties in with the 'lasagne phase' that I, and so many of us, experience in times of grief. Lots of hearty food and over-promising of help. While people are in this phase, they refuse to believe all this help isn't sticking around. Surely this re-remembering of the true purpose of humanity and all of this kindness is compensation for what they have been through?

People often assume that this is where we see 'humans at their best'. In the immediate aftermath of major disasters, I have been bombarded by TV researchers asking me to come on local news and talk about how amazing communities are. But I never do, in case I overstate what we are seeing. Which is a human rush to comfort, which will soon be followed by a societal need to move on. I know that very soon, everyone else will leave the broken place or person behind. This is very true of moments in our personal life too. One of the most common themes in grieving, is how, after just a few weeks, people can feel abandoned. We cannot go on making lasagnes forever. It's not realistic. At some point, people will go back to their normal lives. But for the person or community who was flooded with support and love, it can feel like a shock, even a further loss.

The slump

Most of all, I know for certain that after the honeymoon comes the slump, which is a sweeping low trench on the next stage of the recovery graph – a time of anger, distress, disillusionment, fragmentation of community groups. The pain caused is no longer slightly numbed. The plaster is off.

In Gresford, when the slump hit, it was exacerbated by actions of the mine's management, which seemed so very familiar to me. The wages were stopped for the men who died from the minute of the explosion and the terms of the donated relief had almost no provision for those who were made unemployed by the pit closure. They had to quickly find work elsewhere. There were long-running disputes about the colliery management and who was to blame, and this reverberated into the clear-up of the site and the management of the disaster fund. In order to literally survive, to keep body and soul together, feed their kids, many of the women – now single parents – had to go out to work. They made bullets in a nearby munitions factory.

And in this case, there lingered one further open wound that, as I have come to realise through my work, never stops suppurating without resolution. As the hundred-year-old interviewee on the *Welcome to Wrexham* documentary spoke about, so many years after the disaster, the families never got a body back. My work has taught me that that sort of forensic uncertainty and ambiguous loss leads to a slump that is multigenerational.

It left the place with a patina of struggle and unresolved distress even I recognised as a seven-year-old some five decades later.

We will be returning to the slump later, as it is a very difficult phase of the aftermath of a disaster. But what is important to know is that under the low, flat line of the slump, invisibly, change is happening – change which can propel you forward into the next phase.

We are still here

Right at the end of the graph comes the magical, illusory uptick. Things are supposed to get better but that is not guaranteed. I realised this was what I was watching for in Wrexham, both in the documentary and in my visits – I have moved back to the area and this is where I take my children out for tea now. It is unusual to capture in detail and with Hollywood Technicolor the delayed recovering of a place. Particularly ninety years later. An uptick put on ice. Maybe I was looking hard for it, but I really do believe we get to see that uptick on screen. But I could see that a place held in stasis for many years had finally puffed out its chest and roared '*Yma o hyd*', which translates as 'We are still here'. It is sung in Welsh at every Wrexham game. It is an all-encompassing response to the threat to survival posed by the mine explosion and the legacy of the disaster entangling with other things, like economic crisis and a generation of men robbed from the community and allowed to remain beneath, without proper rites. *Despite everyone and everything, we are still here.*[5]

On the graph, the uptick is only ever depicted as a little flick of a tail and that's where the graph ends, but the years of afterwards are implicit. Is a place or person then recovered? It can also bring with it its own problems. If they recover 'too well' outwardly, it can lead people to believe that their disaster was, in the long run, a positive thing. This is a particularly cruel commentary that has been subtly present in reviews of the disasters that I have attended, particularly those that have hit deprived areas. Sometimes the changes are so profound and the regeneration so well resourced that I am asked if that means the disaster was beneficial. I flinch every time at the question, that marginalises the many years of hardship and misery that the residents or the person have endured.

The uptick which looks so neat on the graph is not straightforward: it's fragile in its early years and can bring its own problems. But with care, love and courage it can usher in a new life. Even in the midst of our grief, we can influence that uptick. We can't undo the disaster in our lives but there are things we can do, and things we can ask for, that may profoundly change what happens next.

The graph is not a steady process, following neatly from phase to phase with a fanfare between each. The pendulum swings back and forward – there is no perfect ending. And this is where understanding the importance of both the need for the uptick in the graph and the power of the graph itself really kicks in.

When stars keep colliding

When we 'officially' train for disaster, we are usually encouraged to focus on one incident at a time and pretend there are no other dominoes to fall, but the Fates don't work like that. It can seem breathtakingly cruel when you watch one family repeatedly get hit with illness or tragedy, when it seems they should have used up their lifetime allocation of bad luck. Sometimes catastrophe unfolds into catastrophe, as though each was inviting the next. Illness or accident can kick off a chain of events like financial strain and relationship breakdown. Life events often hit the same place hard, over and over again.

The States of Jersey, in the Channel Islands, suffered multiple tragedies in 2022, all in the space of a few weeks. On 8 December, three people died on a fishing boat, *L'Ecume II*, that sank after a collision with the state ferry. The captain, crew and craft had held a totemic role in the local community. Their loss was felt acutely.

Just two days later, a gas explosion tore through a block of flats in the island's main town of St Helier, killing ten people and scattering their belongings to the cliff edge and into nearby woodland. A hundred other people would say goodbye to their homes forever.

And a couple of weeks later, a further fifty families were also forced out of their homes in the Grand Vaux region just north of St Helier by flooding.

And then a fourth blow from the Fates: an outbreak of unknown toxin, possibly botulism, hit herds of Jersey's iconic cows, killing one hundred of the animals.

There was not one explosion emoji on their recovery graph, but several, all in one month.

I had visited Jersey several times in the years before, always under more peaceful circumstances. The States of Jersey ran their disaster response training in the island's hospice. I would sneak off at lunchtime for some air in the garden. As a course trainer, if you don't actively hide in the disabled loo or behind some bins, people will bring their questions to you mid-toilet break. I have learned to be necessarily wily.

Hospices strive to be calm and beautiful places. They are popular venues for my sort of training. Sitting in that garden, with its planters with herbs and various benches, what hit me was how their work and mine are near-identical. Their deaths may be cleaner perhaps, the surroundings less sooty or hazardous, the goodbyes a little longer. But each is still an interruption to a plan, a before and after in a number of lives. They too navigate an aftermath. The workers there knew the same thing as me, that all we really have is today.

Before the disasters, my most recent visit to Jersey had only been, presciently and awkwardly, eighty days before the trawler sank and it had been joyous. I had gone to the island's Festival of Words event to celebrate the publication of my book. In a marquee dressed up like a big top there were fairy lights and tables groaning with cake, and a green room packed with fascinating people.

My event had been sponsored by important women of the island and several government figures were in attendance. One had shaken my hand firmly and repeated the phrase I hear a lot, alongside a nervous laugh, when I introduce my work: '*It's lovely to meet you but I hope we never see you again. You know ... for work reasons.*' Fates rattled. She would see me again for work reasons, just a few short months later.

The States of Jersey made a call they did not ever want to have to make and asked me to come and talk to them about how to manage the scene and the personal effects. It hurt that this next visit would be so very different. No fairy lights this time. The collision of bad stars always changes places, changes people, however much we stubbornly try to pretend they don't. Like a toddler who will not be strapped into their car seat, we briefly refuse to believe that we will allow anything to be different. We want the life before and, by God, we *will* have it back.

Arriving in the earliest phase of disaster, what the graph calls the honeymoon phase, is fraught with emotional danger as a responder and I have learned to time my visits incredibly carefully. I don't mention the graph, as a rule, at this point. It may be too much, too soon, and the messenger will be well and truly shot.

But then I was invited back for the third visit, the one where I do talk about the disaster recovery graph. It was a couple of months later and a weary Servisair man reached for my suitcase. I made my way down the metal steps from the plane to tarmac, shocked into breathlessness by the cold air. A taxi driver asked why I had come and I lied, telling him a vague story about business consultancy. I bored him until he turned the radio up.

I located a cup of tea and then gently told a room full of hopeful people – police officers and local government councillors and people in charge of the state's bank accounts – that they and their place were changed and that the strange, incongruous euphoria they were currently experiencing would not last. That the global outpourings of solidarity and support and allegiance were not really real, but a stage in the graph that no place, neither beautiful nor desperate, can afford to believe in.

They fought me, wanting to convince me that theirs was the one place where what I was seeing around me was here to stay. The knitted hearts, the JustGiving funds, the children's posters were all enduring and infinite. It was personal. The majority of those lost and those now living in temporary accommodation were residents and there were kinship connections with them.

But all it usually takes is one of these lantern bearers to say quietly, usually about halfway through my time in the room, that they have started to see signs of the slump already. Then the floodgates open. That is why the timing of my third visit is always so crucial. People need to have seen the first blight of the slump before I get there. Suddenly, there is a realisation of the comfort that learning from a thousand earlier communities' experiences will bring. There is also a realisation that their hard work must go on alongside the ups and downs of the graph. In Jersey, the leaders and professionals in that room began to see that they would need to do the heavy lifting of moving this place forward within the slump. They would need to talk about tourism and trade while the flowers were still piling up outside the town hall. In that moment, there was suddenly a shared understanding of what it would take to bring this place through to the uptick.

So far, I have not found a community for which the recovery graph does not resonate after a crisis. I think that some of its magic is in the way that it depersonalises the struggle. There is unification in knowing that you are treading a path walked before – so often, so commonly, in fact, that others have written about it, and then others have written about it again, and then all of that writing has been turned into templates, like the graph.

I have been interviewed for glossy fashion magazines and been hugged in draughty church halls. Spiritual moments where people have reached for my hands, tears in their eyes, to say that it was something they did not know they were waiting for. Big professional bodies of people introduced to the disaster recovery graph for the first time have been hungry to know more. After listening to me talk about it, the Royal College of General Practitioners dedicated space in their Christmas newsletter to expanding on it. I think it spoke particularly to primary care doctors because they are so often the first responder to whom people say, out loud, that they are in the slump. Their patients talk around a set of non-specific symptoms and their blood work comes back normal, but *something isn't right*. And they just keep coming back to say it. The graph allowed the GPs a new perspective on what was happening. And of course, another element that made it even easier to adopt as a tool was that after the pandemic, the general practitioners were inside their own slump too.

Trusting the promise

I occasionally meet an older person, in their tenth decade, who insists that their lives have never been touched by fire or brimstone. They say that all they had ever really known as a family was peace. No lost babies, no financial hardship, never affected by serious illness. House never flooded. No out-of-control chimney fires. At most, their car had spluttered to a halt on the motorway, but that was quickly resolved. But that kind of life is an exception.

Most people will experience unwanted change or loss at some point in their lives. Sometimes it will feel very surmountable, but at other times it will divide our lives into the time before and the time after. This can be true of events, but it can also be true of feelings and relationships. You can forget that help and allegiance and ways to get through are out there, that there is light in the dark.

The greatest gift that the recovery graph has given me is clarity to ready for a very long journey ahead. In society, nothing is permanent and the walking in footprints has to be done over and over again. But to know that there is a path and that there are people who have walked before, who know the way – well, that helps. That small uptick at the end of the line shown on all recovery graphs represents a promise that things will get better.

As I watched the town of Gresford sing out its Welsh anthem to survival, I noticed something that I have spotted when observing many disasters in so many places. The interest the world showed in the place of Wrexham was the necessary accelerator, the fuel, for the uptick. Neither places nor people can start to feel better or get better without interest and compassion and love. These things provide the oxygen for the rebuild.

Showing that interest a little more deeply can have great value. The doctor that follows up with a child's health. The neighbour who continues to bring round meals to someone in illness. The teacher who gives a star to the child going through turmoil at home. The friends who listen to your breakup story for the thousandth time but then move the conversation on to more hopeful things. What makes the difference is the knowledge that progress may be slow and the slump may be long, but that there are people willing to walk alongside you.

The lesson here is that there is a path – but also that the path can't be rushed. In our lives, we desperately want to get to the uptick and, perhaps more harmfully, we want others to get there too. We want to rush them past other, uncomfortable and confronting stages and get them to just being OK again. But that takes labour and hours that simply have to be put in.

If you can, value the time that the path takes. Use the time to really make sense of what has happened and what comes next.

It's bloody hard work but use the graph as a handrail. And if somebody else is walking the path, remember the difference that love and continued, careful interest can bring. And that it all starts with one step.

Your recovery kit

Plan your diary like an emergency planner.
I think of the year in quarters and I am tuned to where we all might be in the seasons. I always harness the 'new-term energy' of September and know there will be a mix of excitement and trepidation around December. For me, January and August can both be quite low and long months. What are the patterns and shifts in your own year?

And then there may be significant dates relevant to your personal calendar. For example, those who have experienced a loss often have a low, physically and mentally, in the weeks running up to the anniversary, so it is always worth being aware of and honouring those challenging weeks, factoring in that you may need rest and headspace then.

Embrace your intuition.
Learn to really listen to your inner voice and instincts. Often, fears about risks will be minimised by those around you but it absolutely can help to explore them head on. Don't be shy about asking for a second opinion or changing your plans.

Look outwards.
Take comfort from the fact that there are many people walking the path outlined by this graph, all around the world, alongside you. We have always known these times and there is allyship and a

college of advice out there. Social media gets a bad rap but it is still an effective way for helping you find relevant causes or people in a similar boat.

Introduce the recovery graph to your employer or human resources department, if you have one.
It works incredibly well in work settings too and can help with developing a much more compassionate approach to things like absence management.

Lesson Two
Taking Stock

Emergency planners learn to watch out for secondary flooding. Residents only realise it is happening long after the ministerial visits have stopped and the TV cameras have moved on. It's a nasty little disaster trick after a place has been inundated with floodwater. When the householder first assesses the harm, they miss the water under floors or creeping into porous walls. Just when you think your household has escaped, when you thought you were one of the lucky ones, your own wooden floors start to buckle and your plaster starts to flake, the water comes up from below. It was there all along. Waiting.

This is why, when a place has flooded, I plead with local emergency planners to not submit the numbers of properties in need of assistance straight away *as final*. Central government is hungry for data in the first forty-eight hours and then loses interest. But sometimes the calls from flooded residents don't come in for six or eight weeks, when the later waves of the disaster hit. Then the mould starts to appear.

We are all vulnerable to missing the true and deeper effects of life's turmoil.

The very first thing that I am asked to work on when the calls come in in the days immediately after a disaster is often the 'impact assessment' – one of the double compound nouns that we use a lot in emergency planning to throw a cloak over a really tough task. In order for any kind of plan to be put in place, the government, local and national, and the communities too, try to work out what they are dealing with. We actually all do it as humans anyway. It's the first bit of data gathering that we do when something goes wrong. 'Show me,' we ask a child when they complain of a graze from a fall from the tricycle. We need to know and to see what we are dealing with.

In the worst-case scenarios, it can seem just too much to form the words. To try and pretend that it can in any way be fixable. But in order for any healing and rebuilding to happen, we have to confront the inventory of what has happened. I have learned that we barrel on through life, rarely doing our own impact assessments or sitting back to think about what happened. But it is essential that first we walk through what has changed.

Aftermath

On 24 August 2016, an earthquake of 6.2 magnitude on the Richter scale devastated a part of rural Italy. The day after, the mayor of the town of Amatrice stated that his town 'isn't here anymore'.[6] The final death toll of 229 was not confirmed for some months, once again driving home the point about the time taken for the impacts to appear. You have to be able to find the dead first. Hundreds of people were injured, and thousands of homes, businesses and local heritage sites were destroyed.

I visited Amatrice a few months later, in January 2017. The television cameras had moved on long before. We were part of a Save the Children delegation sent to review the ongoing 'work of recovery'. Children had been particularly hard hit by this disaster (as they so often are) and when we arrived, many were living in temporary accommodation, the majority of their safe places lost. There was snow on the ground and the bleakness of life after disaster was sharpened by the harsh cold. Snow covered all of the temporary buildings housing the life-scapes of this place. These temporary cabins are often so similar the world over – shiny floors, grey walls, temperamental portable toilets. A table tennis table.

The legacy of the honeymoon phase was still visible. Fraying signs stating 'Amatrice will stay strong'. But the pain of the original disaster had by now been compounded by the revelation of a series of building scandals which had meant that the buildings were no match for the strength of the Earth's plates under them. I am so used to these nasty whiffs of scandal that follow every disaster I see. As predictable as a working clock.

The man from the Italian fire service was young and pumped up and did not want us there. This was his home, and as soon as we gathered around him, I could tell he was not comfortable with what he was being asked to do. He had been asked to show us the streets and made us wear yellow safety hats. We were disaster planners from around the world and therefore here for worthy reasons, so I reminded myself that we were not disaster tourists as we piled off the minibus. We would not take selfies at his site. But we would take awkward, sneaked photos that made him glare at us. He used his discomfort to power his legs and strode yards ahead of us. All around us, the few remaining houses leaned at skewed and perilous angles. Earthquakes create scenes that are like children's drawings. We could only marvel at the level of destruction before us: churches and municipal buildings with just a single wall still standing or a jagged brick edge around a sole, defiant doorway. Our yellow heads looked like insults against the beige, gold and snow-white scene.

I could not pull my eyes away from the once-were-houses. Rows and rows of them flattened. The compacting of the many materials and fabrics reminded me of the most fragile wafers of choux pastry. Thinned concrete, layered on the scraps of bright fabric that had been curtains. Somebody chose those curtains. Girders, wires and a single shoe.

The responders hoped that they had recovered all the remains of the missing but they couldn't be sure. By this time, it was five months after the quake but the impact assessment was still in its earliest stages. Neither the responders nor we, the new violating visitors, had properly taken stock of what the disaster had done. The sense of ambiguous loss pervaded. Cars crushed, trees crushed, souls crushed. There was data, yes – lists of houses and other types of buildings lost; they knew how many people they had in temporary accommodation – but the town was still trying to count all the other losses. I have seen enough responses now to know that many of the impacts are too intangible for a spreadsheet.

The fireman had not yet found the words to talk about what had happened to his town. I have learned that coherent narrative is rarely possible in the first year. And sometimes for many years after that. Instead, he lost his temper with a member of our delegation, an enthusiastic, cheerful and big-haired woman from New Zealand. She had fallen behind the rest of us and as she stumbled and tripped to catch up, she began to giggle nervously. He exploded. He had been waiting for a reason to do this, like a shaken Coke can. He let rip in broken English about respecting this place. The woman looked like she might cry, once she had sunk into the ground with humiliation, and I felt desperately protective of her.

The angry fireman didn't know that he had so much more in common with her than he realised. This woman was here with us to share her own insights into the human side of impact assessments after earthquakes. She was from Christchurch in New Zealand – one of a handful of places where I have got to know the area both before a disaster and after it. At 12.51pm on Tuesday 22 February 2011, Christchurch was hit by an earthquake of 6.3 magnitude on the Richter scale. Although this was actually an aftershock from an earlier earthquake on 4 September 2010, this latter shock was profoundly more destructive due to its proximity to the Earth's surface.

The damage this second time was catastrophic, with whole suburbs being destroyed; 185 people died.

She and the Amatrice man had both lost kin and homes. A few years before, she had been introduced to disaster recovery in a way that she too wished she had never needed. She knew better than any of us about the suffering that he was still in the process of absorbing. She wanted to tell him that what comes next is even harder than what he had been through already. People who have lived here for decades will leave this place, the physical rebuild will take 100 months, not the promised 10. There was no mocking or malice in her laughter. But the fireman never got to see her as an ally.

People inside their own disaster may have little patience or time to learn from those who have walked the path before. They have also been through so much that their skin feels flayed and raw, and their eyes plead for no more bad news or hurt. But if the fireman had been able to listen, he would have found people who would have been able to talk him through how to breathe out. To help him find ways to articulate what comes next. This is true of all of us and may also be one reason why we struggle to learn lessons from past events. I often wonder if there is a comfort in there somewhere about pretending that something is unique and just happening to us.

Hiraeth

By the time I visited Amatrice, it was well inside the disaster recovery graph's slump and the fuller impacts were still becoming clear. There was nothing left: everything would need to be rebuilt or brought back in. I knew from bitter experience that what would be fashioned back into this place would never be quite the same. All of the special places had gone – the churches, the museums, the restaurants where people had celebrated the baptisms and toasted the dead.

This feeling is *hiraeth*. It is a Welsh word that speaks to a heart sickness for something that is not coming back, cannot be got back. A loss of the life before. I see *hiraeth* everywhere now after the pandemic. In bereavement. In people's sense that they are missing something from their relationship or the way they used to be able to do their job. *Hiraeth* is unfixable. It is just there. When people first hear this word, I often see a strong reaction, as it puts a finger on something that they had been trying to sate in other ways. Attempting to fix the gnawing, nagging sense that something is missing through too much shopping, excessive cleaning, overeating. It gives people a word to describe previously indescribable loss. The Welsh had known it all along.

Although *hiraeth* is an echo and a heart sickness, it can also be broken down into something more tangible. Something you can work with. Not recognising it can cause you to flail around for things to blame. The curtains aren't right, the job isn't right, the relationship isn't right. Something is wrong and you can't quite work out what. Families rehomed after disaster will reject choice after choice, sometimes legitimately, but sometimes simply because home does not feel like it did before.

Understanding and tackling head on the knowledge that the old life is gone allows you to see that there is something that can be rebuilt.

You can lose people through a disaster in many ways. One impact I have come to know well is that people will stick with the town or village for a while, but when the heartsickness at the slowness of the recovery gets too much they leave. Some disaster survivors have told me that they could just about cope with the pain and the loss of the life before, but what finally drives them away is the noise and the dust of the rebuild. In Amatrice, many months after my visit, there would be slow, fragile signs of the infrastructure uptick. Nine months later, my friend and colleague Leanne sent me her research notes and I noted that where I stood months before there was now a food court. 'You can now go for a coffee, meal or even buy souvenirs and local produce,' she wrote. The sounds of construction were everywhere. After disaster, these sounds dominate at least the first three years, longer, sometimes. Almost intolerably noisy and dusty.

That's why I never believe a conference presenter in the first few weeks of disaster, a city's mayor or chief of police, who states proudly 'everybody chose to stay'. *Wait and see*, intones the little alarm in my head grimly. Post-disaster emigration leaves places decimated, and then outside people stop visiting too.

In our own lives, one of the biggest emigrations after life-changing events will be in changes to friendships. People don't always want to stick around for the new you, even if they sent flowers when the initial event happened. Marriages and partnerships break down. A man might feel that since his heart attack he knows he is grumpier and warier. He hates his new sense of vulnerability and mortality, and he knows his partner has started to wonder where the gregarious, life-and-soul, party-starter they fell in love with has gone. The mourning that comes with chronic illness, the loss of the vivacious life-liver, can be as hard as the physical symptoms themselves. It also comes with a hefty dose of regret that we didn't do more when we were able. We fight for a way back to what was before, but part of the taking stock is knowing that was lost.

Ink on paper

Over the last decade, in the UK and many other countries, the central government has demanded, as literally the first action, a list of everything that the tragedy has touched. There is some logic to this. A blank community impact assessment is just printer ink on paper, but filled in and done well it can be the key to a deeper understanding of what this disaster has done. It is the first step in forming a coherent narrative and saying out loud *what this is*. And crucially, it starts a dialogue amongst communities and responders about what comes next.

The impact assessment not only involves counting the dead and tallying the destruction of buildings, but also trying to say out loud the psychological harms and the ways in which you and your place has been changed.

Completing this as a person from the outside, brought in to assess, means trying to guess at what was there before – the elements of community that have disappeared. What was it that mattered to people that has now been marred? What is left? What is gone? This is hard enough in a disaster with a physical site, but vanishingly difficult in a situation where the visual clues are hidden and there are no obvious smoking craters – as, for instance, after a pandemic. You need to know about the place before.

Like many emergency planning tools used in the early aftermath, these assessments are written by responders and not the communities themselves. The community, at this point, is still reeling in shock. Sometimes still putting out the fires. So from the outset, they can feel excluded from their own disaster.

There can be a certain amount of triumph captured in the early impact assessments done by the police and fire services. If there are no dead and limited casualties, or the initial response feels like it has been particularly heroic, the impact assessment will be imbued with such a sense of relief. *It's not as bad as it could have been.* It can feel like a small 'man v nature' victory. This means that the assessments end up being notoriously unimaginative.

There is a resistance to adding to the list of harms that should be included, as if it's unnecessarily moany and just not cricket. My generation grew up with this attitude from our caregivers, which had perhaps been thrust upon them by being children marinaded in a life after the Second World War. I have found that our global colleagues sometimes mock this strange stoicism from the British after disaster – 'Yes, you may have lost one leg but you still have another one,' they will say in a terrible English accent.

When it comes to personal, individual tragedy, a bereavement or crisis, our friends and family around us can do something similar – a toxic positivity that minimises the thump of the loss, listing the ways that we should feel grateful. As somebody who experienced several baby losses, I very nearly committed murders over the phrase 'you can still get pregnant again'.

Intangible harms

In the corner of my office stands a pile of impact assessments, supplied by responders from tens of tragedies in recent years, their completion assisted by advice from me. We start with the central circle of the bang and work outwards. The first questions are normally how many dead and how many injured. One recent one starts simply with 'How many people are affected by this emergency?' Oh, where to start with that one ...

On Sunday 4 March 2018, two people (and then several other emergency responders) were exposed to a military-grade nerve agent in Salisbury. Sergei Skripal and his daughter Yulia Skripal were found seriously ill on a bench in Salisbury, although it was not at first clear who they were or what had happened to them; it was initially reported as a drugs overdose. Mr Skripal was a former Russian agent, and tests showed that they had both been exposed to a substance identified as coming from the 'Novichok' group of nerve agents, a particularly feared weapon that causes havoc with the human nervous system. This type of chemical agent tends to be deployed as a liquid.

Personnel based at the nearby Defence Chemical Biological Radiological and Nuclear Centre, Porton Down, identified the type of weapon used. It was confirmed in a later statement in the UK Parliament that this was a novel Novichok, not previously seen before. At least two other police officers involved in the investigation also became unwell, one extremely seriously. The effects on him and his family continued for years afterwards. He battled not only ill health but still lives with the trials of trying to survive something about which so little was known.

On the same day that the local responders declared the incident response was now over, a tragic further twist of malignancy occurred. On Saturday 30 June 2018, two people, Dawn Sturgess and Charlie Rowley, were admitted to Salisbury District Hospital having been taken unwell in Amesbury. Dawn Sturgess died on Sunday 8 July and counter terrorism policing confirmed the link between this incident and what had happened to the Skripals. It is believed that Sturgess and Rowley had come into contact with Novichok via a perfume bottle that Charlie gave to Dawn, although quite how this happened is also a matter of ongoing inquiry. Quietly, because the government does not like to admit to its international enemies that something big might have happened, whole parts of towns were shut down again. Dawn and Charlie had been at a church barbecue just a few hours before, so all the furniture and bunting from that was seized and destroyed.

Across both incidents, a total of fourteen sites were identified, with twelve requiring decontamination activities to be carried out. Twenty-six agencies were deployed and the initial physical clean-up took over a year. Recovery groups were set up at national and local levels to address all aspects of recovery, including community engagement, economic recovery, public health, remediation and communications. I was asked after the first year to review the impact work and by the time I got there, the nerves of both the community and the responders were frazzled. If our enemies' plans had been to test us a nation, it's fair to say they succeeded – not that our politicians were going to let the Russians know that. People were being asked to live alongside a completely invisible killer and trust greatly in the quality of the response.

It was clear that the formal impacts of these events had been assessed in a militaristic way (several of the partner agencies were military units), with an emphasis on science and technical solutions. The harms that made it to the spreadsheet were tangible – houses, the contaminated ambulances, Yulia Skripal's pet guinea pigs, some of the injured (more would emerge). But when I did my work, I wanted to tease out the much more intangible harms. I was there to review the work being led by local government and local public health but, as ever, this turned into an incident that had a lot to teach me.

In many ways, this work, which was still being completed at the time that calls started to come in about a strange pneumonia in China, was the most effective preparation for a pandemic I could ever have had. How we would struggle to reconcile the very scientific with the deeply human. How responders would be begged for assurances of 'total safety' that they could never give. There is a lot written in the risk management literature about how hard it is to fight an 'unseeable' harm – infection, nerve agent, radiation, a new virus. Something that is hard to picture and grab at, to fight head on.

In the Novichok cases, I was schooled by the indefatigable local Director of Public Health Tracy Daszkiewicz, who is the perfect mix of broad knowledge base and compassion. Directors of public health in English law are responsible for much more than people realise. They are there to respond to physical and mental ill health issues in the community but their work is also supposed to be preventative. Heading harms off at the pass. Tracy and I are kindred spirits and end up in equal amounts of trouble at different ends of the country as we try to get people to think more bravely about the effects of whatever disaster we are currently faced with. We both worked hard on making the case for a much broader range of impacts that would need attention and mitigation.

Tracy had lobbied hard for an assessment of the long-term effects to local people in the Salisbury and Amesbury area and for the response to stay as human-focused as possible.⁷ Her extensive training and background in disease outbreaks and working with disadvantaged communities greatly informed how she thought about the impact of this thing that was both so new and yet so familiar. Disasters hit unequally and almost always pummel those already dealt an unfair hand.

The incident in Amesbury which led to the death of Dawn Sturgess robbed a daughter of her mother and impacted people already living on the edge. Dawn was living in a hostel for people who had been homeless or were being supported for addictions. This led to police speculation that she too had been a drug user, something the inquiry later said there was no evidence of. Tracy was worried that this gave the state the chance to minimise and write off some of the impacts. Dawn was perceived as being somehow worth less to the state and, wrongly, less likely to be missed. Both Tracy and I picked up on a distasteful relief coming from some responders that at first the fatality appeared to be getting minimal attention in the press. I cheered when Dawn's case was picked up by renowned lawyer Michael Mansfield, known for championing families' rights after tragedy.

Another thing Tracy had pointed out was a slightly prudish tone to the business impact assessments that were being demanded by central government who then devised a grants scheme for Salisbury and Amesbury (some of the forms designed would go on to be used nationally in the Covid pandemic). They were happy to support the daytime economy but the 'naughty' nighttime economy – the strip clubs, the gentleman's clubs, the sex workers that lit up parts of the towns at night – were all omitted. It was something I had seen before. We tend to look at the approved impacts of an event, but maybe shy away from the ones that we think are more taboo.

In our own lives there are things we feel allowed to say and then impacts that we keep hidden. The impact of a physical condition on our sex life, the debilitating stress-induced constipation, the impact of a virus that did not kill us but robbed us of our self-esteem and any sense of joy. We tend to take stock of certain harms but not others. We also stay painfully censored by a societally imposed hierarchy of who gets to suffer most. We rate 'being alive' over all else without true regard to the fact that we are here but may not be living.

Finding the harms

Just as with an impact assessment in the case of a disaster affecting whole communities, for all of us as individuals, the very first step on our path is to take stock of what has happened, including all of the intangible harms. I often notice that people will tell me proudly, and as a badge of honour, that they are doing great after a demotion at work, the ending of a special, important love affair, a period of illness. They have bounced right back. But if you ask those around them, they will have noticed profound changes. I think it is one of the reasons why we stand back and stare a little at a friend when they have been through something. It's a way of trying to assess the damage. I notice it all the time – we grip someone on each arm and say, 'But you are looking well!' to reassure ourselves more than anyone else. (The ones that really flummox me are the friends who say to each other, 'But you are looking slimmer'. Phew, one good thing about the awful life event, then!)

It is the family around the person who will often be much more honest about the behaviour changes – whether the person is withdrawn, angry, distressed. My friend, a social worker, told me that he thought he was really 'bossing' his response to the pandemic: working hard, impressing his managers, still managing to rescue children from violent homes. He was pretty sure that he wasn't taking his exhaustion and his shock and his horror home with him. And then he heard his little boy say to his wife, 'But we don't have daddy any more; he is somewhere else.'

Clearly, it was a moment to look at what had happened full in the face and take stock, ferreting out exactly the toll that the events had taken.

Quarrying intangible harms from life's events can sometimes take quite a lot of work. It can help to write down some of the things that have changed or been impacted after events – if that doesn't feel too depressing. Gentle probing often reveals that things people may at first not be giving any space for are actually really important to them. Feeling low. Feeling like you are missing your old life or missing out. No impact is too small to record. An impact is an impact. Anything that is affecting you, no matter how small, deserves a place on your impact assessment.

Often the longest, most drawn-out tail of any event lies in the psychological impacts. I feel grateful to live in a time when this is so much better understood. I cannot imagine what it must have been like to be struggling in times past when conditions like 'shell shock' were so misunderstood and only whispered about. My great-uncle froze if he ever heard a Japanese accent or a mention of Japan after his time in a prisoner of war camp. My dad's colleague, a history teacher who had also served in the Second World War, would dive for cover whenever he heard a loud bang in the school corridor. Another thing that an impact assessment never gives enough weight to is the affect on someone's sense of safety after a traumatic event. I am not sure that ever comes back.

There also appears to be some link between poorer mental health in survivors and the promotion of certain narratives in the media that initially paint those individuals as heroes and saviours, perhaps linked to pressure of expectation and also constant exposure to particular parts of the story. I always urge organisations to dial down those early, ultimately cruel 'hero' narratives but they are catnip for journalists.

Then there is toxic guilt, a particular blight for both responders and survivors of crises, both in large-scale catastrophe and closer to home. Especially in loved ones whose family members have died suddenly or unexpectedly. This is another of those unspoken harms we forget when we take stock. People really beat themselves up that they were not there at the end or that their attempts at performing resuscitation on their loved ones did not work. They torture themselves with ways they could have done things differently.

Unless you sense-make, often with some help, you turn your pain inwards and can go mad with thinking about what you might have been able to do differently. It is particularly painful to see this theme come up repeatedly in a narrative around why someone later took their own life. Blaming yourself and feeling toxic guilt manifests as many things in the survivors left behind – denial, insecurity and low self-worth.

There are things that can be done to address feelings of toxic guilt – which can arise in everything from how a divorce may have played out to bereavement. Hone an inner voice where you are kinder to yourself. Work hard not to torture yourself for having what can feel like 'forbidden' thoughts, such as feeling relief that the very ill person who you cared for has now died. Allocate that tomorrow will be a guilt-free day and just practise that for a few hours.

Accepting that some things are now very different may well be one of the hardest parts of taking stock.

Watching for the ripples

As responders, we forget certain demographics in 'official' impact assessments all the time. We might forget infants under two, lumping them in with 'children' when in fact the vulnerabilities of tiny babies and particularly their feeding needs are very different. Or think about children but analyse their needs through adult eyes. We forget people with additional needs, particularly when they are not visible to us. We forget lesbian, gay, trans and non-binary people. We forget people who don't speak our language. We miss out Romany and other travelling communities. Then there are communities that we other, like refugees and sex workers.

Disasters have a substantial ripple effect, and the list of those affected can quickly grow and reach far into local, national and global communities. The idea of ripples across communities was first defined through research by A. Taylor and A. Frazer, two psychologists who produced a classification of a disaster based on factors such as proximity to the impact zone and psychological consequences of the disaster experience.[8] They were writing about their observations of the aftermaths of an air crash, and were trying to emphasise that these events had much wider implications than many in society realised. Their 'ripples' included not only those injured (physically and psychologically) and those bereaved, but others who may be involved either as witnesses or responders, both in the short or longer term: 'This highlights that the line between victims and non-victims is not as obvious as might at first appear and that beyond those who have been hurt physically – or who have incurred losses of possessions – are a wide variety of "hidden victims".'

Groups affected broadly include bereaved, survivors, responders, witnesses, local community and then what responders often call the 'wider community'. That phrase 'wider community' feels ever more capacious and elastic in an age in which the globe feels ever-more connected. A Lebanese community in Luton may feel just as impacted by an event in Lebanon as by an incident in the next street, but early impact assessments often miss these communities. As well as the psychological effects, these far-away communities may also suffer tangible physical effects too. A loss of family members, a loss of financial support, a loss of a sense of home.

Then there are the 'communities of circumstance', a diaspora of people who are connected by the experiences of the event. The friends of Dawn and Charlie. The air crash survivors who have come from all over the world, but who, because they were all on that one plane, will forever have that connection. All of this means that ultimately, even smaller scale incidents can affect thousands of people all around the world.

In big disasters, these ripples are always messy, but, as with so many areas of emergency planning and response, we attempt to bring order to it. One way we do this is to put it into Excel spreadsheets with a plethora of technical jargon and acronyms. I remember with some horror the first time I realised that responders were cramming all of those affected by the Grenfell fire into one acronym: BSR for 'bereaved, survivors, residents'. The shortest of reductions to describe the biggest of challenges.[9]

I have never seen an early impact assessment completed by responders that considers something like intergenerational trauma. That the children not yet born will know of this thing. That it will ripple down the generations. We are beginning to live in a time when the effects on those who have survived conflict and genocide are better understood. Its slowly becoming recognised that what may have happened to our parents and grandparents will cascade down to us and perhaps our grandchildren. A strength comes with naming this and saying out loud what it is. Giving it validity in your list of impacts.

It is always worth looking at the ripples of something that you are going through, or someone else is going through, to see whether you are accidentally minimising an event or bringing the circle of consequences in too close. You may be making assumptions about the ties that bind or the time that healing takes. In illness, we can underestimate the time to both physically heal and mentally recover.

Following a bereavement, we often minimise the effect of losing friends who are not 'blood family', when they are actually our special 'chosen family'. We also tend to play down the loss of pets – though I am grateful that my career has coincided with a growing awareness of the ripple effect of losing a much-loved animal in a household.

One recent incident saw a school caretaker killed and the school children felt his loss acutely. He had been in charge of a lot of the noticeboard displays and had even played Father Christmas in the school fair. The children didn't want anyone else to play Father Christmas going forward. Initial impact assessment conducted by the police and the local authority had no way to recognise this hidden impact. The children raised it when they were eventually listened to.

Ultimately, the very nature of trying to capture something on a spreadsheet glosses over the fact that we are all individuals. The impact assessment is the very start of a process that collects all those ripples together and tries to unify them like jigsaw pieces that simply cannot be wedged together. Like so many of the tools that sit constantly by my side, I know it is imperfect, but I also value it as a building block – the first, necessary step on the route to what comes next.

Assessing impact takes regular check-ins and the acceptance of frequent setbacks. There is a balance that has to be struck with how often a place is revisited and scrutinised. But at the same time, it is important not to see what comes next as neatly linear. Appearances can be deceiving and places can have an initial and superficial bounce back that does not last. It can be strangely empowering to understand that it is normal for things to feel as though they are getting worse, or to find new, undealt-with things suddenly appearing. I was moved recently to receive some new guidance on supporting children after loss that reminded us as responders that one of the times that loss can be most profoundly felt is at special events, many, many years later. At graduations, landmark birthdays and proms. There were suggestions on how to ensure that children who died could still be honoured many years later by their peers.

The castaway effect

So what can we do with all of this in our own lives? How can these tools often used at scale by disaster planners offer guidance as to how to approach the aftermath of the individual crises and traumas we will experience?

I asked around amongst emergency planning friends to find out how they approach an impact assessment. All of those who are involved in mass casualty and mass fatality responses spoke of how the very first thing you have to do is get beyond your own shock at what has happened. Take just a moment to ground yourself physically. Shock is necessarily numbing but stops us doing our best thinking. Denial may also be playing a part.

I did not realise how potent and genuinely hallucinogenic the denial phase of grief is until I lost my dad. I still see him everywhere – my actual dad, not somebody who looks a bit like him. I say hello to men on the street, I reach out to strangers, and then the Dad avatar melts away. It has made me really distrust my previously loyal, hardworking brain. It renders every day as groundhog day. This leads to something we emergency responders call the castaway effect.

The Tom Hanks movie *Castaway* hit US movie theatres in the Christmas of 2000 and was released on DVD just three months before the terrorist attacks of 11 September 2001. Hanks plays a FedEx employee whose plane crashes in the South Pacific. He ends up trying to survive on an uninhabited island. The first time I heard the description 'the castaway effect' was a year later, when responders to 9/11 were briefing the team I was working with. The effect alluded to the way in which the bereaved of the World Trade Center, particularly the children, passionately believed that there was a chance that their loved one had escaped the inferno and somehow got themselves to Staten Island. They were adamant: their parent was living somewhere else, maybe confused. This was not a hope or a whisper, this was a certainty that their loved one had survived and they scoured for sightings. Then they saw them on every street corner. It took a long time for them to face a different reality.

Sometimes the taking stock is artificially delayed by well-meaning responders. In the aftermath of the Grenfell fire of June 2017, I learned about how modern technologies may be inadvertently elongating or playing into the denial phase. I gently counselled my concerns when young health workers offered to recreate, using virtual reality technology, a home that had been lost so that the person could find comfort with a headset on, pretending to sit within it. I have also seen a concern that I raised over a decade ago come to reality with the use of cooling technologies applied to the cots where hospital workers place stillborn babies in a room made to look like a nursery. When these were first rolled out, parents were sometimes encouraged to keep their lost children there for several weeks and care for them as if they had been born alive. Other professionals urged that this could cause a confusing rush of mixed emotions and allow a false hope to set in as well as confusion about what was real and what was fiction. Occasionally, the cooling mats would be accidentally switched off at the wall and the baby would begin to rapidly decompose. The reality would hit fast and hard.

Now the advice is more nuanced and the time limits for the cots have been shortened. The days of whipping a deceased newborn out of the arms of their parents are hopefully long gone, but there is also a middle ground that has to be found. We have to say what this is.

Getting out of 'fixity'

As I have become more practised at completing an impact assessment with both reeling responders and communities, I have become more skilled at making them talk and encouraging them in the 'stock take', though they still wince and struggle. It is a process heavily entangled with the 'denial' that comes with grief.

One way that I can gauge where a room of community members is at is whether they can simply tell me what has happened, using words like 'dead', 'has died', 'gone'. Often, many look at the walls, pick at their cuticles, dab their eyes or leave the room. It takes a long time to get them to shape the coherent narrative, forming the words on their palate. I also urge that we go gently here. Whether it is a gathering of stunned townsfolk after a flood, or someone picking their way through the days after the loss of a loved one, sometimes the taking stock feels like a stinging slap across the cheek or a bucket of ice-cold water, forcing someone to confront difficult facts. The part of taking stock is accepting, once and for all, that the thing has happened.

I have found that this requires time, quiet and emotional space. The work of Dr Yael Danieli is useful here. She is a trauma psychologist who works extensively with survivors of the Holocaust and of genocide.[10] She used the term 'fixity' to describe the state that many of us may find ourselves in after significant shock or trauma. Bad stars, big or small, can leave us stuck or fixed, with our thoughts mired in strong glue (one of the most common things people say that makes me realise they are in a stage of fixity is that they have stopped being able to read for pleasure or even at all). The effects clamp at our throat and our chest. I have sat with many people with this psychological glottal block – absolutely nothing travelling through the vocal cords. Or I think of other people, ebullient and wired, trying to convince me that nothing bad has happened at all. There is no room for 'trivia' or 'frivolity' – we snap at small talk and find ourselves zoning out to life's normal noise.

While some people are just very, very angry, like the fireman of Amatrice.

Danieli examines the harms caused by staying rooted in fixity for too long, which may make the trauma effects even worse. This makes me feel a bit better about the need to ask people to do this. I have learned a lot about how the stock taking, the unfixing, is done. And I have learned that nothing else can happen without it.

Start with making a list. When something happens, you and your kin have to be truthful and stark. When you're taking stock, never be too optimistic and consider as many curve balls as seem possible. Also essential is that you keep checking back in as things continue to change.

The best advice on starting the process of taking stock came from my friend John, who endured the loss of his mum and dad during the pandemic, and his sister just before. He wrote something that helped me and other colleagues profoundly – an article that reminded those of us who work with death that what we thought about grief is fundamentally challenged when we suffer our own losses.[11]

John initially resisted conducting his own impact assessment. He was determined to out-run the multiple disasters that had hit him. He had wanted to be somehow inoculated from the physical effects of grieving because of all that knowledge and experience. He had even grown up in a funeral home. But grief still found him.

It was grief counselling that eventually helped. First, his counsellor found that he had the inability to focus on a task, stay on a topic, and was procrastinating. John then went on to suffer with one of the most common side effects that I encounter in my work amongst the bereaved and disaster survivors – a profound intolerance of 'trivial' things and particularly of questions that seem so unimportant and meaningless: *don't you realise that the worst things that could happen has happened and now you are asking me about the washing machine spin cycle?* It is something I have been particularly aware of in my own life because it is so hard on relationships and on family life. After difficult times, we so often are grumpy and intolerant and hasty.

Like me, John has looked to his work as a form of solace in darker times: just two days after his father died, he insisted on teaching his University of Bath undergrads by Zoom from his parents' house. He has no recollection of the content of that talk but reflects that the outpouring of love from his students 'saved him'.

And this moment also taught him something about taking stock, taking a breath as the first stage of the impact assessment. 'You have to talk,' he says in the article about what the last few years have taught him. 'So, keep talking . . . That is some of my key advice. Talk as much or as little as you want – but talk the way you want to talk. And keep talking.' Which also means that you have to make space for somebody around you who is struggling too. Allow them to talk, while you properly listen.

If this resonates with you, then the first step is to make time for the process. The impact assessment needs to be given credence and respect. Stop everything else that you are doing and put the kettle on. It's time to talk.

Your recovery kit

Watch out for the spiral.
Sometimes you can find yourself in a vortex, looking for reasons as to why something has happened or demanding to know why things are so unfair. Now is the time to get a handle on that in a very deliberate way. I will often start by saying to a room who are rightly demanding this level of clarity that there is no reason to it. It is unfair. Those

are truths that have to be accepted. This does not mean that you have to accept that there is nothing you can do about it. It also does not mean you should stop finding out about the event or asking for apologies or learning. But it might mean that you have to pick some of the battles or work out what is possible for you.

Find your place to take stock.
This might be a cafe or a library or a park. It might be quiet or bustling – whatever works for you. Consider writing your thoughts down while you are there using a mind map or a sketch pad.

Put the 'agenda-less' meeting in your diary.
This works well with a team so consider it if you are a manager of people. I have worked with a number of organisations who have been using this technique after a violent or traumatic event at work. It's not the same as a formal debrief; it's a timetabled and deliberate afternoon off, usually in a venue away from work. With good cake. Don't mix it with other business; it needs to give people time to just say out loud what's been happening. Consider some gentle, external facilitation to help with getting the conversations going.

Compartmentalise your campaigns.
In my work, I meet a lot of people fighting for important causes and they often ask me for advice

on how to keep going and keep sane. I always advise to try to bring some separation to their work. People end up with papers and newspaper cuttings and angry letters piled up next to them at home, leaving no time or space for them and their family to shut off. I am very careful about putting away any material relating to difficult work. I also apply this approach to difficult things at home. Medical letters and financial material have places in drawers and boxes. This does not need lots of room. Just a couple of good document carriers from a stationery shop so that everything can be put away out of sight until the next time you choose to engage with it.

Enlist help.
A brave act is to consider the appointment of a burnout monitor – somebody that you trust very much who is able to tell you the compassionate truth about how you might be changing in front of them. Mine is my mum!

Taking stock involves processing and letting go of failures and disappointments.
This is important because they may be linked to the things you are recovering from. So often, I see people being incredibly hard on themselves after major life events. It is important to think about how you talk to yourself here – we may often have a very critical inner voice and tell ourselves we are

not good enough. This is of course damaging in a number of ways and stops you from taking stock accurately. We will all have different ways of dealing with our inner critic but it's important to actively try out different approaches to dealing with yours.

Value fallow.
This was a lesson I learned early on in emergency response. If you suddenly have a quiet afternoon never, ever fill it with work or chores. Any quiet day before a storm is a precious day. Go to the cinema.

Do breathing exercises.
There are various ways to approach this. The one that works for you will be quite personal. I have been taught several in my career. The overall aim is to slow the physical symptoms of anxiety, calm us and re-oxygenate. At times of stress, we often breathe in a much more shallow way, leaving us de-oxygenated. Try to do breathing exercises every day so they are second nature when you most need them. You can literally do so anywhere, so there's no reason not to!

Count every impact, no matter how small.
When finding the harms and taking stock, try not to overlook anything. And do avoid comparing them to anyone else's experiences. Don't be

influenced by a hierarchy of what you think should be harmful or that someone else 'has it much worse'. You are only placing barriers in the way of your own healing.

Lesson Three
After the Honeymoon

My childhood home on The Wirral (never drop the *The*) was just a few miles from the Hilbre Islands, an archipelago of tiny islands that would be cut off several times a day and night by the River Dee. The nature reserve is a haven for ground-nesting sea birds and seals. The whole place is only accessible by foot and there are strict rules governing access. A friend of Mum and Dad's had a lease on one of the tiny cottages and would allow us to stay for a few nights in the summer holidays. There was no TV and you could only live off what you could carry over to the island. My sister was much braver and more agile than me and would spend hours scampering up and down rocks and scooping sea creatures out of nets.

It should have been magical. But as a young catastrophist, I could never truly relax due to a perpetual dread that one of the four of us would become trapped in the quicksand that encircles the islands. Maybe it was the influence of 1980s children's television, but I was acutely vexed by this thick mud which was a perennial hazard on the walk out to the islands. I was on edge the whole time.

Being stuck in mud seemed a particularly horrifying way to go and the billboards of advice and talks from local rangers did not help. 'If you struggle the mud sucks you in harder – you might even break a leg from the force of the pressure,' they proclaimed, as my nine-year-old eyes widened. Occasionally the local newspaper, *The Wirral Globe*, would carry on its front page a story of a local trapped up to their middle and then hopefully rescued by a Royal National Lifeboat Institution crew with hot tea and mud boards.

As I have come to know, the slump after a disaster, when the 'honeymoon period' is over, is very much like quicksand. When things happen to a place, like a serious flood, the signs of the slump can appear as a physical 'greyness'. Rubbish may be piled on street corners and people seem to walk with invisible sandbags on their neck and shoulders. Nothing is right and every public meeting ends up in tears and shouting. On an individual scale, its often made obvious when you notice that somebody has stopped looking after themselves or their surroundings. People will look fatigued and there may be sudden weight loss or gain.

But is the slump all that it seems? I have also learned that there is something going on underneath the sand – a complex mix of powerful and necessary forces, hidden by the greyest of times. This is when the rebuild is unexpectedly nurtured and what you do in this period really matters. It can feel so relentless and, most of all, so pointless, but I have learned that it has purpose.

Underwater

On the night of the 20 August 1989, Andrew Sutton looked up and saw a monster with big, black eyes coming straight for him.[12] Andrew was twenty-eight and a graphic designer in London. That night, he had reluctantly agreed to attend a friend's party. The monster he saw was in fact the *Bowbelle* dredger that ploughed into the much smaller *Marchioness* party boat at 1.46am, on board which hundreds of people were celebrating a twenty-sixth birthday party on London's River Thames. Official reports show that the *Bowbelle* weighed 1,880 tonnes and was more than 260 feet in length. The *Marchioness* was 85 feet long and weighed 46 tonnes. The size difference between the two was colossal, with the tiny pleasure boat being described as like a toy, no match for the hulking structure that submerged it. Twenty-four of the drowned victims were found below decks; the remaining twenty-seven were recovered from various parts of the Thames over the coming days. I have met a number of survivors of that night and they all talk about the cold and the dark of both the night and the water. The big, black eyes were the holes in the bow that cables ran through, but they haunted Andrew's dreams for years.

Fifty-one people drowned that terrible night and many others were physically injured. Tens more were left to work through this complex, fraught disaster on their own. Andrew Sutton managed to escape from the boat and was eventually dragged from the water. The next few years for Andrew were heavy and blurry. They were also lonely, tainted by a kind of wonder that the rest of the world didn't seem to be able to see what he and his fellow survivors were going through. For many of them, it felt as though they were stuck for years inside the terrible events. Survivors have often described the feeling to me as being as if you are walking around looking at everyone else through a window. Life for many in a situation like this can be punctuated by flashbacks, nightmares and trying to avoid even leaving the house. And in 1989, there was even less recognition of what people might need after a traumatic experience than there is now.

Andrew's slump was elongated by a cruel legal aftermath. Inquiries requested and denied, criminal charges collapsed. He described later how this fraught aftermath of the *Marchioness* collision affected him. Campaigning groups lobbied for an official inquiry into how an accident like this could happen in the middle of London. But a public inquiry into the accident was refused by successive transport ministers. A later report by the Marine Accident Investigation Board was criticised by relatives and survivors as a whitewash. Eventually, allegations of manslaughter against the skipper of the *Bowbelle* and the ship's owners were brought only to be dismissed for lack of evidence in 1992.

Criticisms of the coroner's office, the crews of both the *Marchioness* and the *Bowbelle*, the Port of London Authority and even the lack of preparedness of the Thames River Police were swamped in a complex legal row that continued until a coroner's inquest finally ruled in 1995 that the victims had been 'unlawfully killed'. Not until February 2000 – nearly eleven years after the disaster – was a formal investigation launched by John Prescott, then secretary of state for transport. Lord Justice Clarke then reported that a formal investigation should have been held earlier.

Andrew Sutton followed all of these events from the sidelines. He could not escape the feeling that in some way he didn't deserve to be part of the 'official' *Marchioness* tragedy. I have come to know many survivors who find complicated reasons to feel not worthy of placing themselves within their 'own' disaster. We do this all the time with things like our own health too – we put ourselves in an imagined hierarchy and minimise our own suffering. We deny ourselves the help we need because we feel undeserving of it. Most commonly, I see people with no physical injuries massively underplaying their right to claim their mental anguish.

Andrew continued to deal with the flashbacks and the nightmares, the chronic insecurity and depression on his own. For several months, if not years, he says, he would find excuses not to leave home, certainly not to travel abroad. When he did eventually venture abroad, he made meticulous plans, checking and double-checking all of the arrangements to make sure 'nothing unexpected could happen'.

In the media interviews that Andrew was finally able to give – twenty years after that night in August 1989 – he talked about tentatively starting to do more. And then, very slowly, he rebuilt his career. He started to work with the bereaved and survivors of the Rwandan genocide. He found that he formed a connection with other survivors: 'What I found is that surviving the river made me empathise with people not just because they had lost loved ones, but because I knew what was happening inside their heads afterwards. That's what I wish I'd had – someone to say that they understood and that I wasn't crazy because I felt anxious, depressed or scared all of the time.'[13]

There are days in the slump when we can't get out of bed. It can hit us unexpectedly just when we think we are doing well. It can end up entangled with much earlier feelings and events in our life. The slump is incredibly difficult to get out of. It cannot be done in one single bound. There is a trick here to knowing you are inside it and that there may be ways to get out. I don't think you can always rely on a profound epiphany but instead look for tiny glow-worm lights on the horizon. They add up to something.

Scaling the trench

There are some disasters following which the slump feels like the Mariana trench, the deepest oceanic depth known on Earth. Despite attempts by authorities to try to pretend that the uptick is well within reach, the aftermath of the Grenfell Tower disaster is one of those where the slump is more overtly not going anywhere and any uptick will always be perilously fragile. There are physical manifestations too of being still inside this disaster for a long time yet. The skeleton of the tower, shrouded in white material, still stands, haunting the skyline.

The fire of 14 June 2017, in which at least seventy-two people died, was the worst fire London had seen since the Second World War. It began in the kitchen of one flat and then engulfed an entire block by 2am. Seventy people were injured and 223 people managed to escape. A large proportion of the dead were from ethnic minority backgrounds. The tower block, part of the Lancaster West Estate, is in one of the richest boroughs in London, the Royal Borough of Kensington and Chelsea. The borough houses royalty, celebrities and government officials, with houses in one exclusive street in the south selling for upwards of £35 million. In contrast, the north of the borough, where Grenfell stands, has a 38 per cent child poverty rate and is dominated by social housing. At the time of the fire, residents had come to fear a programme of gentrification and marginalisation. The highly flammable cladding had been put onto their building, their homes, to make it look better from the outside.

This disaster is one of the few I have seen where there was no honeymoon. It hurtled straight into utter misery and despair. Its incubation phase is relevant to everything else that has happened since. So many of the survivors and bereaved, and even the dead, had warned the authorities of the problems with the tower and the likely scenario that would play out that they barrelled straight into anger, a breakdown in any trust, divisions between groups and paralysis about what to do next. Any idea of healing has become inextricably linked with a need for a sense of justice and truth, something I have very rarely seen achieved after tragedies the world over. The misery of what was allowed to happen, the utter failures of the state and the building sector who allowed such dangerous products to infiltrate this and many other builds, pervades all that we try and do as responders. At the time of writing this book, an inquiry report that took seven years to write has concluded that nineteen companies and fifty-eight individuals can be considered as 'suspects'. There is little clarity on what that means will happen next.

Susan Rudnik is a local resident who lives in the shadow of the charred remains of Grenfell Tower. She is a renowned art therapist and immediately put this work into practice at home. Straight after the disaster, alongside a number of other residents, she started building a children's art psychotherapy charity a few metres from the tower itself. They 'occupied' a disused community centre, the Henry Dickens centre, in the days after the fire and eked out a community centre, youth club and play events. Anne, who now cooks thousands of meals for children a year, literally took the keys hostage from the council in order to be able to access the place. Anne is a local matriarch, small physically but a giant in stature. The first staff meeting was held in Susan's garden. Later, she and her colleagues expanded the work into an outreach programme across twenty schools and nurseries and an adult service, including a partnership with

Age UK for older residents who also found the therapy beneficial.

Susan was raging the first time I met her. We were both guests at an event in 2018 about how to make residents feel a bit better. She had asked loudly and stridently for access to the same advice that I was giving to the council and the National Health Service. She argued that this should be every community's right.

She told me to meet her for coffee so she could hear more. She practically hoovered up the disaster recovery graph. 'That makes sense,' she said quietly. I spoke frankly about how I thought the communities of this place were deep within a slump that would linger for a long time. It was the first time anyone had been honest about that, she felt. 'I was glad I knew about the slump,' she muses now. 'Otherwise it would all have felt so relentless and so personal.' Everyone else had been promising a recovery that was just around the corner. But understanding the slump allowed Susan to depersonalise the struggle and to plan ahead.

I asked Susan what living inside the slump feels like today. She laughed bitterly and said that it is all they know. *Every day is the bloody slump.* But she has also learned to recognise the tiny green shoots of fragile hope and the better days.

Most of these fragile shoots come from the children themselves. I have noticed that people have often found a future and a source of hope while working with children. Several of the police officers who responded to the destruction of the Indian Ocean tsunami of 2004 went on to raise funds for new orphanages and children's charities in Thailand and Sri Lanka. I often wonder if this is linked to children being a totem of a possible future that's worth fighting for. Animals too are magnets for those struggling out of quicksand and are particularly acknowledged for the role they can play in men's mental health. Having something to get up for every day, that is completely reliant on you, forces you slightly forward.

For decades, disaster responders have tried to lay down advice for what recovery looks and feels like. After the earthquakes in New Zealand, this was taken forward by responders there, with a lot of support from the New Zealand Red Cross and Australian Red Cross. This collection of responders produced a guidance document that I often draw on, and I showed it to Susan. It's a summary of all the principles and observations that helped them during the long work of coming back from these events.[14] That often things would feel like they were getting worse not better. That tensions and fall-outs would be inevitable. That you can overinflate your sense of indispensability and start to feel that you are the 'recoverer', stopping other people from flourishing. It's a simple document but it travels, and Susan says that it helped a little. She felt more empowered. Her family, the charity, were slightly more ready for the lows – the anniversaries, the disappointments, the inquiry report that seem to open up new sub-trenches.

Latimer Community Art Therapy at the Henry Dickens centre, a cacophony of voices and play, is one of my favourite places to go. Children hurtle round a table tennis table or shake off flour from making play dough, while others use clay, paint, ink, paper to try to make sense of their experiences in quieter, private spaces.

Watching the local people grow this charity, with intense emotional labour, late into the night, made me reflect further that there is something much more active happening inside the slump than it often seems. It is a busy and brutal time, but necessary too. I realised that the slump may look stagnant and viscous as a stage, but it is also a chrysalis for what comes next, building the membranes of what needs to happen if a place or a people are going to survive.

I have learned that when this fraught regrouping is done, it may lead to a much more loyal and resilient tribe. It's a sandblast of an experience that lays a foundation for the future. Torturous as it is, I have come to wonder if it actually contributes towards a stronger rebuild, with more robust roots.

The emotional labour in these hard times can feel too much. We might only be able to manage very small bits of action, but, together, collectively, they add up to something. Each time someone makes a meal for others. Each time a new good memory is made. These are all little pieces of solid ground to stand on as you look for your route through and out. One of the greatest privileges of my work is getting to watch all of the little moments that happen during this time. They are much more covert and strained than the grand gestures and outpouring of solidarity that happen in a honeymoon period, but so vital.

Hurt and division

That's not to say that the slump isn't incredibly painful when we are deep into it. We will all have known this place at some point in our lives. I recognised I was in a slump when I was struggling to carry a baby to term. My relationship with my husband, Tom, suffered as we found separate ways to process the grief. Then there was a further pressure as family members tried their best to say the right thing.

I have so often seen this sort of fragmentation in the wake of disaster – strained family relationships or tensions within communities as groups that formed in the first few weeks start to fall out with each other. Different parts of the communities, or our families, will challenge what they perceive as slights or cruel thoughtlessness. Small behaviours really start to grate.

A common division seen at this point in a big disaster is actually between the bereaved and the survivors – groups that outsiders will often lump together as having lots in common. As I learned early on, they actually may be feeling very differently to each other. Many disasters end up with multiple advocacy groups, all with slightly different names, and, at the beginning, they fight with each other more than anyone else. Often, they don't ever find coalescence, though what I do tend to see by the seven-to-ten-year point is a sort of grudging respect for each other. But this fragmentation allows a necessary, albeit painful, laying of everybody's cards on the table. When the disaster is personal, some friendships end in the wake of it, but the ones that last are stronger and tighter than ever. I have learned that this fragmentation needs to be allowed to heal slowly and tenderly.

Then there is the anger. Hot rage at things both big and small. There is overwhelming exhaustion, fatigue and the start of the post-disaster somatic symptoms: gastritis, respiratory tightness, strange rashes and insomnia. The body trying to process the enormity of what has just happened. Life can start to feel utterly relentless, not least because there is so much to do in the aftermath of disaster. Things don't happen one challenge at a time but come crashing in, big and small. Domestic appliances often seem to just 'know' that you are trying to hold all the threads together and, before you know it, the washing machine has spewed its half-washed and sodden content over the kitchen floor. Or the cat has sprung an abscess.

Then there is a sense of betrayal often manifested in a feeling that people around you have let you down. When you need colleagues or family the most, they appear to fade away, usually just as the workload seems more insurmountable than ever. Hurt is such a potent factor in the slump, as you start to realise the failures that have happened all around you and how much of the common platitudes after loss or big life stressors mean very little. You may feel misled by the honeymoon phase. A thousand problems appear to be caused by terrible slights or livid jealousy, but actually it's usually much simpler than this: you are hurting and often the other person does not realise. For this, there is only one answer: you have to let that go. Hurt is a corrosive emotion but the acid only burns one way and that is onto you.

In limbo

As Andrew Sutton found, one factor that also further elongates the slump can be the legal aftermath that accompanies so many of life's events. The trauma of separation, dragged out by difficult divorce and financial wranglings. Bereavement only compounded by 'sadmin' and the insensitive bureaucracy that goes with it. Fighting for your right to a specific cancer treatment, being earmarked for redundancy and sorting out a care package for an elderly relative are all processes in which the timetable and processes are set by someone else. We are currently seeing people wait two-to-three months for a date for a funeral and families having to endure thirteen months before receiving a scientific report on a child's death. There is a nearly two-year delay on inquests. Family court processes may drag on for a decade. The very definition of limbo.

What a time in your life to realise just how big a fight is ahead of you – between you as David and the state as Goliath. And sometimes another party, someone you once loved, too. The wait is exhausting and creates a stasis within the affected people that simply cannot be broken.

In situations such as these, it can feel impossible to move forward, in any direction. Every decision seems to be the wrong one. But some decisions taken much earlier than someone feels comfortable with can make a positive difference in this time. There is of course still a balance to be struck and a definite caveat here – I do completely agree with advice to not make any major, hard-to-reverse decisions, such as a house sale or retirement, until a few months after the initial trauma and also to ensure you are seeking help for the effects of the original stressor. And yet, it's an important part of this lesson that what can feel too soon, can later prove to have come just at the right time.

Find your mud boards

By virtue of living near the quicksand of the Hilbre Islands, we did meet people fairly regularly on The Wirral who could recount tales of how they got stuck and got out of it. One thing that always struck me was that it seemed to require herculean effort and strength. And it's similarly true that the only way through the slump is really hard graft. Communities and people have to start doing things that they really don't want to do much sooner than they want to.

To get out of the quicksand also usually requires great allyship – often the actions of a friend where life's lottery has meant that their wellington boots are still on solid ground. In The Wirral, stories told of how people would hold each other up for hours, cupping heads with hands until more help arrived. Finding allies has been key for me when climbing out of the slump.

The Grenfell art therapist Susan battles every day the trauma of what happened to her, her family and her community. But she found a way to keep going through helping the children of this disaster. Over the last almost eight years, often with substantial intervention and support, she has seen them laugh again, collect exam results, travel and, most importantly, find the words to say what was done to them. Those things help.

With extraordinary bravery, Andrew Sutton went diving to meet his monster head on. He swam down to the *Bowbelle*, which had since been sold and renamed before it broke apart and sank to the ocean floor near Madeira. The monster was now a wreck, filled with fish, and he was able to touch it. He cried, and right then something changed.

Many ancient belief systems held that you had to return to the thing that hurt you, lie within it, place your injured parts next to it to discharge the toxic power it held. I always think of the families of those who died in the Lockerbie air disaster in 1988, who asked to lie in the holes that had been made when their loved ones impacted into the earth. Responders thought they were mad, but I have always understood it and I have seen it several times since. Many modern approaches to trauma build attempts at 'total avoidance' of the trigger but I have always found comfort in something a little more direct.

I have thought a lot about ways to simply keep going through this time. I have come to know that the first, most important is to recognise it for what it is: the slump is a grinch of a time, an absolute bastard. Once you realise you are inside the slump you need to look for mud boards – the solid objects that will provide something to hold onto and, eventually, form part of your route up and out of the paralysing quicksand. These don't have to be yours, but I know these are the boards I need laid out ahead of me to find a path through the mire:

- See your situation for what it is and recognise too that it has some purpose for regrowth.
- Take stock – as we discussed in the previous chapter, do your own impact assessment.
- Get your health checked. There can be other reasons for struggling in hard times and one of those can be your health. It is so important to be aware of the possibility of things like iron or vitamin deficiencies, or an underactive thyroid. And talk to clinicians about things like menopausal symptoms. In the pandemic, I was guilty of blaming everything on the disaster slump that I knew so well, when in fact what was needed was a hearty dose of ferrous sulphate. This is also very true for mental health as well. So, get checked out.
- Don't overlook the basics. It is almost so obvious that it makes it easy to forget when faced with quicksand: get some nutritious food inside you and, as far as you can, rest.
- Look to who else needs help. Susan and Andrew both found their way through the slump by turning their energy outwards and working with others. Altruism is a great way to start seeing a horizon, a

life afterwards, and also gets you out of the house a few times a week.
- Lean into the extreme discomfort that comes with trying to de-slump. Force yourself, if you are able, to get outside or make one new contact. But ready yourself for the exhaustion and distress that may accompany that.
- Cherish, notice and sing out loud the appearance of any green shoot.

Whenever I am deep inside my own slump, I put on as loudly as Tom can bear my favourite song, my funeral song, 'You'll Never Walk Alone', as a reminder to just keep going.

Your recovery kit

Plan for your own slump.
And for family, friends and the community around you to slump too, depending on what disaster you are facing. Don't bear a grudge if the help and the rush to support dries up. It's natural and expected. If you have any reserves, share them.

Improve your sleep.
Try to improve your sleep patterns if you can at this time. I love the research by Professor Maiken Nedergaard that equates sleeping with a 'deep clean' of the brain. Her team described how the tiny channels in the brain work in a similar way to

the lymph system in cleaning out molecules that need to be removed. Focus on sleep quality by avoiding screens for at least two hours before bed and sleeping in a dark room. People also find it helpful to avoid caffeine in the second half of the day. Daytime routine is also crucial here – getting up earlier and also getting outside to expose yourself to all-important daylight.

Be present.
Sometimes, you need to quieten your brain and just be with those around you. This is definitely something I have had to practise and still get wrong. Actively listen – phone down and away, notifications silenced, TV off. The best people to train me in this art have been good funeral directors who would never do a meeting with a family while also checking the football scores on their phone.

Lesson Four
Needful Things

You have ten minutes to flee from your home to an emergency response centre. What five things, that you can carry, would you grab from your home?

When this question is posed in quiet, ordered, non-emergency settings, people take time to muse and to work out both what is most precious and what is most practical – house keys, phones, wallets, changes of clothes. They then carefully outline the one item that is 'irreplaceable' because of the memories stored within – it used to be a photo album, but often now people say their electronic tablet or iPhone.

I have seen the real answers to that question play out all around the world: a woman who grabbed her pet cockatiel in her cupped hands (no cage or food, just the bird). Children who went for their electronic gaming equipment but not their medicine. People who arrive at an emergency shelter with their phones but not their phone chargers (although we can usually find someone who will share). I have seen many people exit their houses in their socks. Or bare feet. Or even without any clothes at all. And definitely without their keys.

For a photo essay in 2022, the *Guardian* asked people from around the world what they had taken with them when they fled.[15] The scenarios included human rights activists fleeing arrest and a woman escaping domestic violence. A common thread throughout the accompanying essay was that people tried to take family photographs with them and documents that signified the most important moments in their lives. Issam, a human rights activist in Gaza, explained that these things were needed to hold on to his history and his humanity. People with slightly more time or who had been in this situation before took their passport and their laptop and charger. People who were hoping they were facing a temporary situation that would be rectified soon took a pillow that smelled of home and forgot their documents and jewellery. When given a little bit of time to think about it, people tend to pack an intriguing mix of items intended to meet a whole bundle of needs in extremis. A link to the life they were running from, a way to stay alive – water and medicine and snacks – and then something to keep worrying hands busy. We see a lot of knitting in evacuation centres.

Small, banal life moments can become big emergencies surprisingly quickly. Every couple of years, somewhere in the country, we respond to a variation of the following events.

A retired gentleman looking to expand his vegetable bed realises his spade has connected with metal deep within his soil. Two hours later, a major incident has been declared in a joint operation between local responders and the military. He has struck an unexploded Second World War bomb that needs to be defused. Technical advice is sought from three countries. Satellite imagery is used to manage a safe route for defusion. Meanwhile it's the local authority's job to meet the basic needs of 200 displaced residents in the confines of a local library, with peeling paint and a loo that may not want to flush.

Hopefully, in the next few days, this incident will become no more than an anecdote for them to tell to friends. If we get this right. But in the meantime, we try as planners to bring practical help. A place for everyone to sit. A tea urn. We have agreements that mean local emergency planners can raid supermarkets for socks, biscuits and Cup-a-Soups. Ideas of how to meet need in our field are often military in origin, so involve cot beds and ration packs and, if you are really lucky, a 'sanitary pack' with some soap and a giant sanitary towel. Our kit boxes are filled with kettles and too-big torches and phone chargers and an inexplicably large quantity of Bic biros. When you join an emergency planning team, an introductory job will be to check the stocks.

But I often wonder if we are paying attention to the right things. Do we know what we really need in a crisis?

Hierarchy of needs

I have found that regardless of the type of emergency, some needs are universal and carry across cultures and countries. Some of these are simple and obvious, while others might be easy to identify but harder to fill, and some are difficult to spot at all.

Emergency planners love diagrams that make simple sense, can travel and can be copied easily on to a slide. Our 'go to' has often been Abraham Maslow's Hierarchy of Needs, which, while being criticised for its rigidity and Western bias, still proves to be a useful framing device. It helps us to understand what humans require to survive and thrive. It is built around a five-tier model of human needs, often depicted as hierarchical levels within a pyramid. From the bottom, most essential elements upwards, the needs are: physiological (food, clothing, shelter), safety (a sense of stability, job security), love and belonging needs (friendship), esteem, and self-actualisation. The theory is that needs lower down in the hierarchy must be satisfied before individuals can attend to needs higher up.[16] So, only when food and shelter are provided, and we feel safe, can we start to meet the other needs, like feeling a sense of belonging or self-esteem.

It interests me that Maslow's ways of thinking about need were being developed in the Second World War. A time, a bit like the period after the pandemic, when harsh light was being shone on how we come back from something. Trying to find meaning and purpose. It seems no surprise that a number of psychologists have returned to the theory in the last couple of years.[17] We know that our needs are not quite being met but we are not sure how. It seems timely to re-examine this.

Thinking about what you need to survive, to come back, is the next step after taking stock. Somehow, we have been drilled that centring ourselves like this is selfish or a waste of time. But what I have learned is that thinking about your own needs at this point and then extending that thinking out to those around you is time well spent. The initial stages of crisis see your mind and body necessarily kick into a sort of protective automation. Whole weeks can pass and you are not quite sure how. But once you have taken stock and got some of the sadmin or necessary rituals out of the way, it is often the time to start thinking about the things you are going to need to get you through. The result will be a highly personalised plan but with a number of common themes.

The door key

The first time I really thought about meeting level one on the pyramid of needs on a massive scale was in December 2004. As 2004 became 2005, emergency planners all around the country were tasked with getting ready for the people returning from countries affected by the Indian Ocean tsunami of Boxing Day 2004 in mass repatriation flights. People had lost everything on the beaches or in hotels. Some were still in swimming costumes when they arrived in Manchester or Heathrow airports. They had literally fled to the airport, still wet and bleeding, with all personal items lost in the angry waters.

When bad things happen, people often just want to get home. For many, when they landed back in the UK, that would be the first time they would properly take a proper breath. As it often is, the 'need-meeting' effort was a partnership between a number of parties, in this case local government, health authorities, holiday companies and airports.

We had a few days to think the plan through. We would meet the tourists' most basic needs first – clothes, food and first aid. Treating the horrible grazes and broken limbs. Then we talked about the other tangible needs and worked our way through the pyramid. A sense of safety next. We urgently needed locksmiths and lots of them. If we could organise transport and get people home, and then through their front door, we could meet this part of the pyramid a whole lot faster.

In any disaster, a door key is always an interesting one for me. If somebody loses their door key we are suddenly presented with fifty other tangible needs to manage. If we can get them back into their house, we immediately find their own resilience reignites. Access to their own things and a shower. Clothes that smell familiar and of home and not of the disaster. (This does not work, of course, for life events that destroy people's houses and also assumes that somebody has a house in the first place.)

The needs at the top of the pyramid came a little later. The online support for those affected by the tsunami was one of the first times a website – now called a 'virtual assistance centre' – was trialled. Hundreds of thousands of people died in several parts of the world that day. Trying to rebuild the sense of self and heal the mind is a need that sits at the top of the pyramid so is attended to last. It is also often undermined by other messaging that we do. That the people affected were 'lucky' to be alive or that things could have been so much worse.

What are our needful things?

I have come to think of our needful things in four categories:

The tangible needs (physical, bodily)

The intangible needs (answers to difficult questions, to feel safe again, to feel confident again)

The impossible needs (for the thing to have never happened)

The hidden needs (pleasure, intimacy, quiet, the need to forget, a last cigar)

They connect to each other and ask different things of us all, which are often more difficult than we want to admit. So I find this framing of the four categories can be helpful and lead to honesty about what needs might be being left unmet.

The *tangible needs* probably are the most obvious: food, a place to sleep, some pills to calm the head or tummy. It used to be the chance to smoke until that got moved into a hidden need. (A few of us older planners can never forget the chaos that came about because the UK smoking ban and the 2007 floods happened in the same month. Somehow, we had to tell thousands of displaced residents in evacuation centres that there definitely was not a smoking area.)

Intangible needs are trickier. I have contributed to a number of media articles this last couple of years asking about the intangibles. People feeling less confident after the pandemic. Less adventurous. More flat. A general sense of 'meh'. We are frightened but are not sure what answers we need. These are fixable, but only after we have taken stock.

Then there are the *impossible needs*. There is nothing to do but reconcile ourselves to the reality that they will stay thorny. They can only be lived alongside, walked with.

For a year, my mum did the 'magical thinking' that often comes with grief, a part of her holding on to the idea that Dad was coming back somehow. That there had been a terrible mistake. She looked like she had been hit when I sat opposite her and said once more and finally, 'He has gone.' The same words I had used months earlier when she had pleaded with me over and over again to call someone who could bring him back. My work meant that I had heard that plea many times before but nothing prepares you for it coming from your own mum. I can take my mum to shows at the theatre, I can make her laugh again, I may even be able to watch her feel joy. But the need to see my dad again will always stay unmet.

At some point in our lives, we will all face the impasse of the impossible need. There will always be times when we can't provide the answer someone needs or make them feel safe again. Some needs will stay firmly unmet and unfixed. I was profoundly struck recently by listening to the wonderful Figen Murray, who campaigns for Martyn's Law after the death of her son Martyn in the Manchester Arena bombing, 22 May 2017. She works tirelessly to improve security at venues and gives regular talks to emergency planners. The last time I heard her talk, she said something that took my breath away. She explained that she would never stop torturing herself for being asleep at the exact moment her child had died. She had seen several therapists who tried to take this guilt away or get her to process this in different ways. But as a therapist herself, she had made what struck me as a brave and profound decision to accept that it was a feeling that would never be taken away from her. No therapy would fix it. It would stay within her for the rest of her days.

Then finally there are my favourites – the *hidden needs*. The naughty ones that I want everyone to know they have the right to feel, though they are often squashed down by societal attitudes and sensibilities. These take some squirrelling out. Some might be very possible to meet, others might need to be pondered on. I love the way that hospices and doctors specialising in elder care approach hidden needs – for a tot of brandy, a quick cigarette. A need to make ashes into jewellery, which is seen as more conventional now but was a highly unusual request at the start of my career. Needs that are individual to the person and their lives that may speak to our desires and the darker stories in our heart.

The need for intense intimacy is one example of needs that tend to stay hidden and undiscussed. Several badly injured survivors have told me stories of being reprimanded by their critical care nurse for getting too hot under the covers with a partner in the immediate days after the explosion or crash. They have whispered to me about a need to feel the oxytocin rush and the connection after something so terrible. It is similar to the baby booms we see after power cuts and declarations of war.

None of these needs make it into the official guidance in the UK. The need for sex does feature in some international humanitarian disaster guides, along with advice to provide birth control, reproductive medicine and antenatal care. It is also present in the bereavement literature and given the term of 'widow's fire' – the need for intimacy as a perfectly natural urge and part of the grieving process. New relationships abound in evacuation centres and even the centres where kin wait for news of missing loved ones. Not always just between those affected but between responders too, and sometimes, wrongly, between responder and respondee too. It has been a source of quiet disciplinary action as boundaries tumble and vulnerability is advantaged.[18] But we don't talk about it.

Pam Dix lost her brother in the terrorist attack on Flight Pan Am 108 that exploded over several miles of Scotland, with the majority of the wreckage landing on the town of Lockerbie. She wrote that her family were made to feel like 'ghoulish sightseers' when they asked to visit the scene and be at the place where Peter was found. I have learned that people expressing their needs can lead to judgement and sanctimony from those around them. Making judgements about whether somebody should visit a scene or spend time with the parts of the body of their loved ones is something I come up against constantly. One of the most common reactions that I get when insisting that a family would like to look at a set of photographs from a crime scene is *still* 'why would they want to see that?' Making the request itself aberrant, deviant and shaming, when it is anything but.

Campaigners for the care of the bereaved and survivors after tragedy have taught me a lot about potentially reframing needs as rights (even if they are not always protected as such). *I have a right to your time. I have a right to this care. I have a right to spend time with that person. I have the right to ask for my needful thing.* My starting point is always that you should not have to explain your needful things as long as they are not harming anyone else. Be honest about your needs and your wants and desires. Don't censor or beautify them.

Seemingly small things matter when it comes to all these needs.

One of the most common requests I get in those first few days after a major incident is for advice on literally *how* to bring people together and the space in which it will happen. I will be told that the first meeting will be in a local primary school. Chairs will be plentiful. But then I realise that the chairs that the stunned public will be asked to sit on are tiny primary school chairs, not meeting the fourth need: esteem and self-actualisation.

Meeting the need is also something that healthcare still does incredibly badly when trying to resolve patient complaints. Aggrieved patients are invited back on to the ward where the original harm was done. Letters are written to the wrong name or address. You have not met the need from the minute someone has walked through the door and all efforts after that point are fruitless.

Missing the moment

Ironically, something that I have witnessed more and more in recent UK emergencies is that we spend so much time mapping 'the needs' and making pathways for them that we actually end up missing key deadlines for meeting them. We miss starts of terms for children or key anniversaries because we are so busy working out the plan or trying to procure the right way to do it.

One of the most frequent criticisms made by official reports into disaster is the time it takes to establish both what the needs are and what ends up being called the 'offer', when those needs are met. Currently, my most common experience in the days after emergency is watching others 'pinballing' as they search for ways forward. It comes from a place of people desperately wanting to do their best in an environment where there is just so much information about how to do it. So the people designing the pathways bounce about looking for the *best* way, the *best* advice, and also bring in more and more people to think about the ways that the needs could be met. The result is that while we think about needs a lot, the actual needs may not have been met at all.

Of course, we do this at home too, rejecting the simple and obvious solutions by trying to research more and more or by insisting that there must be a different fix or a technology that can solve the problem for us. I'm sure most of us are familiar with that feeling of inadvertently creating ten new little problems while trying to fix one big one. This is a common phenomenon within families. In order to meet an older relative's care needs, we will strip them of their agency or introduce a new risk into their life. We forget to consult the person themselves. At some point, most of us will face the juggle of the balance of the conflicting needs and will be faced only with a series of Hobson's choices.

I have also noticed more and more that we flip the pyramid in modern life. We worry a lot – and not wrongly – about children's long-term need for esteem and self-actualisation, but without always considering that we can't get to any of that before we have addressed whether they have had breakfast. We make accessible wellbeing apps for children who don't have a mattress or clean linen to sleep on. The reality is that meeting the physiological needs – full tummies and a warm bed – allows the conditions for the other needs to be met too, to start to grow.

A patchwork quilt of needs

When needs stay unmet, or unexplored, I tend to see longer-term problems fester under the surface, well into recovery. Sometimes, a particular event will trigger a real crisis of unmet need and show just how serious it can be to leave them unaddressed. People have been left to struggle with their memories and their traumas on their own over a period of decades. For the survivors of the

Hillsborough disaster, a football stadium crush that killed ninety-seven people in 1989, the crisis of their unmet need came many years later. Some had survived not just the initial terrible day but the many legal injustices that came afterwards.

The original disaster is one I know very well. It marked my initiation into wanting to work with people after terrible events. The survivors passed their experiences on to their children, who grew up knowing and feeling the disaster too.

Then, years later, on 28 May 2022, at the Champions League final between Liverpool and Real Madrid, a series of errors by both the Parisian police and UEFA forced Liverpool fans into a near-identical crowd crush, straight out of the pages of 1989. I had always wondered how history might have been different if earlier disasters had had camera phones, if the decades of fighting to prove the truth of what happened – counter to spurious and deeply prejudiced media 'reports' – had not been necessary. And here I got my answer. Things would have been profoundly different. Not only did the footage (from all parties) align with the fans' accounts but it also captured something else. It showed the fans, a large number of whom were men – older, young and young boys – rhythmically rocking together, whispering like a Welsh choir not to push forward. 'Don't push.' 'Don't push.' It had the power of a call to prayer. The fans used their deep knowledge of 1989 to essentially keep themselves and each other safe, thirty-three years later.[19]

But it came at a price. When they returned home, local public health teams saw a spike in deteriorating mental health and suicidal ideation particularly in the menfolk of Merseyside. New, strikingly similar events 'trigger' the traumas of the past and, without support, the men had no way to dial down their reactions. Their Hillsborough trauma, unresolved, was igniting and amplifying their Paris trauma.

The local public health team looked to act, alongside survivor support groups. It turned out that many of the men had never previously felt able to talk or been offered the support to help them do so. Although some support had been offered it was partial and accessing it often did not fit with ideas of 1980s masculinity. Having the chance to be heard, in 2022, really helped them. The various therapies offered, including trauma therapy and eye movement desensitisation and reprogramming (EMDR), also proved successful. This was an illustration of the necessity of acknowledging past traumas and experiences. It was also a powerful example to me that survivors of past disasters could still benefit from new therapies and new ways of thinking about trauma many years later. Humans are delightfully complex and carry all sorts of life experiences in their minds and their souls. They get sewn together into a huge quilt – the sum of that person's life experience that grows and grows. People carry their past quilts with them. There is no homogeneity in how an individual will respond to a new disaster for precisely this reason – they will bring to it their past experiences and the ways that they have found to cope.

Thinking about anxiety

I am grateful to live in a time when the role played by many life experiences is more fully understood and recognised, and there are organisations to help with unresolved past experiences. I have a special relationship with anxiety and suspect many planners do. Of course, we contend with it just as everyone does but there is a particularly potent remedy that comes with being able to say many of our fears out loud. I have really honed my tribe in recent years and am blessed with many mentors and sponsors with whom I can sense-check anxieties.

I often think that people who are not in my working world are done a bit of a disservice, in that things they have every right to wonder about, list or muse on are dismissed as 'anxieties'. It is what you do with those worries and how you allow them to affect you day to day that is the key here. Planning, preparing and readying are all good fixes for more mild anxiety, alongside making lists and allocating a small amount of time to think about the list itself and more time to actually tackling it.

As more and more people have discovered the applicability of disaster recovery, I have talked in many settings and one that has become particularly familiar in the last three years has been secondary schools. Schools and the relationships between parents, staff and students have been profoundly affected by stop-start closing during the acute phase of the pandemic and a lingering sense of an uncertain world prowling beyond the school gate. One of the things that has jumped out at me is how often the thick fog of anxiety hangs heavy in the air. Sometimes, teens would be walking nearly bent double and I noticed how hard they were to make laugh or smile in my talks.

It was obvious that these young people *and* their teachers *and* their parents were near-paralysed by anxiety but also fear of responding wrongly to the anxiety in each other. I have been really helped here by the work of Dr Lucy Foulkes who is a psychologist looking at social development and mental health in adolescents. She has helped me to understand the balance between pushing people too far into doing things, while simultaneously recognising that some resilience comes from doing things that scare us. Understanding that anxiety can be reframed into the feelings that go with doing something brave can be empowering and helpful.

She does, of course, recognise that there are some situations that may be harmful and should be avoided, and in some cases that may include a school setting. And that severe anxiety that gets in the way of living life will often need specialist help. It is really important to understand when anxiety might be becoming a problem for you and often I measure this in how much it is limiting you.

How to identify your own needful things

One of the great things about working in emergency planning is you get to see lots of new and innovative thinking about need, which you then get to bring home and practise in your life and in other contexts. And one thing I have learned is that the pyramid of needs might not flow sequentially but instead comes at us all at once, in a sort of carousel.

Two of my colleagues, Jolie and Elizabeth (wonderful women whose spirit sparkles from them), created something that prompted me to think about need in this way. To help with those early difficult conversations about the recovery graph and the slump, they developed a series of flash cards to use with people who were responding to others in need.[20] They showed me that needs must be met in at least two ways – by both addressing the practical and '*the feels*'. In other words, we need to look at the body, but also at the reasoning, the spirit and the soul. Like Maslow, they suggest that the best way to do this is on a full belly, and they give so many different types of need a weight and a point.

Their 'calamity cards' are a wonderful mix of reminders, probing questions, startling affirmations and truths that you didn't know you needed. They use quotes from emergency planners all around the world, but the cards work for all of us in all sorts of scenarios, allowing us to think about all the needs at once. They remind us to get some rest and some food. But also to remember that hard times are really tough on our closest relationships. They remind us that there are limits to what we can do with our time and that no afterwards is ever without its slump and its precarious chasms.

I sprinkle these cards on the tables when I work with both responders and with communities and its fascinating to watch their resistance to them initially.

People don't want to be asked to audit their own needs. Grown-ups don't need flash cards. They will turn them over or try and hide them under their other papers. But as the day goes on, the cards start to speak to them and they learn about why I like them so much. They might offer to read them out to the group. I watch their eyes widen or glisten as they find one that particularly resonates. Sometimes, they ask me if they can take that one home.

One way to build personal resilience to any crisis is to think and talk, just a little bit, about it in advance. Everyone can think like a planner. People assume that emergency planners are obsessed with the scenario detail – what type of tanker will crash and where – while, in fact, we are more interested in the consequences as they are much more uniform across *any* given scenario. So you don't need the specifics of each disaster, as you will always have a similar set of needs.

So think about the needful things of future you. Start with the practical things so that you can be assured that some basics are covered. This means that you might have more capacity to think about other needs later on, should the worst happen. Here are some examples:

- Are your documents and passports very grabbable?
- Do you need a basic hospital bag ready to go for you or your children?
- Do you have a torch in your home and do you know where it is?

- Can you back up special memories and photos to both an online cloud and an external hard drive and keep it at a family member's house?
- What medicines and other aids like spare reading glasses do you need close by?
- Always travel with a phone charger and on a flight keep your payment card, house key, phone and passport on your person and not in your luggage.
- Can you build up a small stockpile of the things you might need in harder times, in advance? Some of that might be tins of beans or a warm winter coat.

Then, with your basic physiological needs met, what else is important to you? What needs make you, you? For me, I have learned how important it is for me to feel listened to and properly heard. I have noticed it in my children too. They want to know that the thing they have said should be taken on board. Most of us feel a need to be seen and to be acknowledged. Our need to be heard and listened to is constantly marginalised in modern life, and particularly in areas like medicine and midwifery. I have learned, at home and at work, that being ignored, shut down and marginalised is one of the greatest harms done to others. It is important to trust your instincts on what you and others in your care will need. Lean into your own voice and your instincts a little bit more.

When I think about my childhood, I realise Mum and Dad thought about needs in a different way to many other families that I met later. They would always frame things as 'what do you need to get to the next step?' It was a bit like living a Mario Kart game, in a good way. They were always bouncing you up to try to reach the mushroom or the coin and access the next level. It would start with a hearty meal and a good night's sleep, no decisions made that evening or while you were still crying about a failure or a source of distress. Then the next day the notebook would come out. The list of needs: what did you need to get from there to there? It's a good reframing – to think of bouncing ourselves up to the next level rather than trying to keep trudging through a list of what is lacking.

Once you know that you have a need, the next step is to try to ensure that it is fulfilled. You often have to ask for that need to be met, something that might need to be accompanied with Destiny's Child levels of sass. I really like the language of 'reasonable adjustments' here, which comes with an attempt at trying to understand different people's needs. I can't drive so I would need public transport and/or a driver. My brain works differently from some other people (I am dyspraxic) so I need to find ways to work with stories and imagery rather than numbers. I need to be heard and so certain types of jobs with certain levels of independence are the ones that suit me. Now, as my health starts to get a little worse, I consider needs in terms of pacing and mapping out the day ahead.

To assert your right to your needful things, be prepared to be decisive. Just like the responders who get diverted into endless lists and pinballing, you may find yourself procrastinating on decisions and looking around for lots of alternatives. Seeking second and third opinions and looking for counter views is a healthy approach, but when it tips over into paralysis and inertia it will invariably stop us moving forward.

Take on board that it is OK to acknowledge all of the various needs you may have through every stage of the recovery graph – the tangible and the intangible – and give yourself permission to go after all of them. Also, be comfortable letting go of things you don't need.

There is one need that I have learned is possibly the most important of all. For people to come together. Humans need each other, and that's a need that transcends culture. Even if you think you don't need many people, some connection is important. It doesn't need to be profound new friendships but little moments of togetherness. We need to chew something over, we need another's smile. Food eaten in crisis should always be eaten together. One of the greatest privileges of my work is getting to see the moment, after disaster, when people realise just how much they need each other.

Your recovery kit

Emergency preparedness.
Have the basics covered so, in case of any kind of disaster, you can spend your energy on more advanced needs. Put a first aid kit where it is easy to grab. Prepare a disaster 'go bag' for if you need

Needful Things

to move on in a hurry. To this, as applicable to your own situation, add:

- Phone charger
- Spare house key
- Medication
- Pants
- Non-perishable snacks and bottled water
- Period products
- Equipment for infant feeding, wipes and nappies
- Any other kits for people with additional needs (e.g. spare EpiPen for allergies)
- Insurance documents (try, if you can, not to skimp on insurance)

Keep the bag in a designated place and check the contents regularly.

If you live alone, think about ways to expand your support bubble and who you can ask for help. Have a plan for short power outages – keep your phones charged and consider battery packs. Your power company has a guide on its web page for actions it wants you to take in an emergency.

Just a note here to be really careful with candles in case of the electricity going out. It sounds obvious but the reality is that fires go hand in hand with power outages. Have torches accessible and extra batteries. There is a reason survivalists wear layers. Invest in thermals and pick up jumpers and sweatshirts at charity shops. If you need to stay warm at home, layer your bed with blankets, throws and sleeping bags, making a nest. Get hats and gloves. Wear tights underneath trousers.

If you are a carer for somebody, you need to get very good at thinking about their needs in extremis.
A worrying situation can quickly become frightening if someone in your house has additional needs. Talk to each other, or to those who support you, about how you would get someone to hospital without an ambulance or whether you would be able to administer life-saving treatment at home, if that's relevant to your situation. Keep hospital bags to hand for both of you. We can all benefit from learning how to do CPR. But also have open, honest discussions when this might not be the right thing to do and plans for when not to resuscitate. There are occasions when CPR will not work. Consider a portable defibrillator if this is a situation you could find yourself in.

Pleasure is important.
The idea that pleasure matters can get really lost. It can feel like its disapproved of or not valued. It's time to move it much higher up your list. Life cannot just be a series of days where you get by. Take away the idea that you don't deserve pleasure. I love the idea that you can actually hone your ability to savour, take pleasure and find joie de vivre. It

is very common after disaster to lose the ability to feel enjoyment – the technical term for this is hedonic adaptation. One suggestion, by psychology professor Sonja Lyubomirsky, is to try to introduce something completely novel into your life. It doesn't have to be a whole new hobby or anything particularly complicated if you are not up to it. Try a new coffeeshop or go for a different walk and try to use each of your senses to savour it.

Encourage connection.
The research suggests that people with strong social connections are less unwell. Technology and messaging apps are great for keeping in touch, but also plan in longer, in-person top-ups so you catch up with others properly. I am always moved by people who are profoundly lonely or feel like they have no one to talk to. This in itself can be a sign of depression. Have a look online for 'how to make friends' and consider whether you have the capacity to do some volunteering. I include animals as people here – rescue charities need you more than ever.

Conduct an anxiety audit.
How are anxious thoughts creeping in and what form do they take? How do you then react to them? What are your particular triggers? You may find them linked to illness or hormones. I find I am more anxious in the days before I come down with

a heavy cold and there is growing understanding of the links between anxiety and our immune systems. Try and avoid the use of alcohol or over-eating when anxious and instead do something that calms you, such as going for a walk or doing something practical with your hands. Being able to hone your inner voice to point out whether something is a thought (everyone hates me) or a fact (I may be a little bit sensitive today) is important here.

Managing overwhelm.
'Overwhelm' is a series of physical and psychological reactions to the mounting sense that we have far more on our plate than we feel we can deal with. Being able to recognise when this is something you are experiencing is vital. Some people become paralysed when everything feels too much and may shut down. My speech becomes more disjointed and I lose flow and words. You may become very irritable, may obsessively clean (everyone knows to duck for cover when I get the vacuum out), or may take on too much and then cancel everything. Work out what gets you back down to a manageable level of 'whelm'. For me, often it's a hug, then making a list with a cup of tea and then complete brain rest. Confide in colleagues and family about how best to support you.

Lesson Five
Bad Help

There are hundreds and hundreds of plastic shopping bags, their handles tied tightly together but their contents still spilling out on to the gymnasium floor. The gymnasium has been borrowed from a local council, but they will want it back very soon. This is now the ground zero of the 'second disaster'. It follows the first with terrifying regularity. An entirely human-created chaos of donated goods. Of pilled jumpers and odd socks. Soiled duvets. Sweat-crisped bras. A bikini. An armless toy soldier.

The initial tragedy didn't do this. We did it in response. It's purely a product of goodwill and of heart. Frayed t-shirts pile up alongside toys that come free with children's fast-food meals. Flip flops and a giant casserole dish with food still encrusted upon it. Responders and local residents are trying to help rebuild a broken community, already working sixteen-hour days. And they also now have to stare in horror at the bags as they continue to spill their contents like sick. My friend picks up a donated scuba mask with a broken strap and the only thing we can do together is laugh miserably. This is a lesson about help in hard times, what works and what really doesn't.

This particular slideshow in my memory comes from the aftermath of a flood in Yorkshire, but it is a scene replicated all over the world. The clearing up of the donated items so often becomes extra work in every recovery I have ever attended. 'Aid' is left to moulder at the side of airport runways and harbours. After Hurricane Mitch, in 1998, planes carrying aid to Honduras were unable to land due to the piles of clothes on the runway that nobody had time to deal with. It can feel nasty and thoughtless, so far from what the donor intended. I often wonder what happened to those kippers sent to the widows of the Gresford colliery disaster in 1934. Did they start to stink?

The urge to help our neighbours is a truly magnificent part of human nature, and in my twenty-four years as a disaster planner I have seen the very best of the human will to do so. But misdirected help often leaves responders clearing up twice. Powered by initial euphoria, people offer up clothes and kitchenware that will almost always become landfill, and what has become described as 'disaster pollution'. The items will rarely reach their intended recipient and if they do, can sometimes make things much worse. Unsolicited items clog up supply chains and take up room on transport. They are often dirty, damaged and unsafe (frayed wiring, loose buttons on a baby's coat).

The horror of wearing somebody else's used clothes that you have no connection to, on top of everything else that you are going through, is even captured in the emergency planners' favourite musical, *Come from Away*, which tells the story of the 6,600 people evacuated into Newfoundland when all air travel over and into America was closed after 11 September 2001. One song expresses perfectly the 'bad help ambivalence' as the 'plane people' are introduced to the donated clothing, accepting that the locals have done a lovely thing but also feeling horror at pulling on somebody else's shirt. Survivors want the chance to wear new items and the self-determination to buy it for themselves.

Survivors of the Grenfell disaster have talked to me extensively about how it felt to be on the receiving end of this jumble. To realise in the darkest of hours that the piles of old clothes were *dirty*. Even some of the underwear collecting at the bottom of a bag. 'Can you imagine what we felt when we pulled them out ... we already knew how the south [of the borough] felt, but now they were showing it?'

Susan Rudnik offers one of her deadpan lines when describing the bottles of water that were deposited hourly outside the Henry Dickens community centre, not asked for, while the tower still burned. 'We had taps,' she remembers wearily.

There was also the horror that maybe the central and local government allowed the donations to keep coming, even though by then there was fifty years of disaster research as to why this was unhelpful. These piles and piles of useless, undignified items symbolise something that, no matter the scale of our personal disasters, all of us will be familiar with: Bad Help.

The first time I properly encountered Bad Help was in the tales of colleagues responding to the Indian Ocean tsunami. Responders fed back horrors from the dockside of containers of pots and pans with broken handles, soiled clothing and expired medication. Some of the containers, sent from well-meaning committees in village halls, had best wishes cards in them from places I knew. As the stories started to come in about quite how unhelpful it was, how time consuming, all around me in England, church halls and primary schools continued to collect.

But the scale of the second disaster here was truly terrible because it was a double whammy of well-intentioned collections and also a much more malevolent offloading of crap from state organisations. Governments also contribute to Bad Help, using the disaster to offload all kinds of detritus, capitalising on another place's misery to offload their expired tins and old, unsafe surgical equipment, while being able to boast about how helpful they have been. I have seen boxes and boxes of kit arrive with none of the plugs compatible with the sockets in the country. A health scandal here in the UK, in 2018, exposed the fact that the UK was sending dangerous morphine pumps, recalled here by our regulators, to African hospices.[21]

Over time, the UK officialdom partially got its act together and agreed to review and reform the way that it donated aid to affected places. The catalyst was the ragged aftermath of Typhoon Haiyan in 2013. Typhoon Haiyan (locally known as Yolanda) made landfall in Central Philippines on 8 November 2013. With sustained wind speeds of 250km/hour and gusts of up to 315km/hour, Haiyan was one of the strongest typhoons on record and left massive devastation in its wake, resulting in loss of life, destruction to physical infrastructure and housing, and disruption of communications, electricity, water systems and transportation. Various types of aid was sent with ranging degrees of success. For example, the vehicles flown in could often not be used due to differing regulations and a lack of training.

The motivation for donating can also be muddled with assumption or prejudice. Barbara Bush, former US President George W. Bush's mother, was captured on camera stating that the help offered to the survivors of Hurricane Katrina as they were scattered to rest centres across the country was probably better than the life they were used to. Prejudice around poverty and the assumption that the gifts we are giving are actually lifting people up from their normal have been a constant in my career. The British approach to help is also snarled up with a colonial legacy and the idea of missionaries and poor little children in low-income countries. Though lately, in a push-back to that, we have seen a growing challenge, a necessary challenge, to the concept of the 'saviour' in charitable giving. Recipients have every right to ask about the motivations behind the help.

Sometimes, wrongly, we want our recipients to be overly grateful for that scratchy blanket and stewed cup of tea – and this is definitely a lesson that carries over to other areas of our lives. Demanding eternal gratitude is a recurring theme in Bad Help. My dad would always say that that nullifies the giving, the helping, altogether. He liked good manners but believed that if you were standing there expectantly, waiting for the person in crisis to focus mainly on thanking you, effusively, then something had gone wrong with the whole interaction. Then you are giving *for* you, not giving *to* them.

One of my areas of work now is training people who will 'deploy' to support families waiting for bad news. These are the teams that are sent to community centres or to airports when someone is waiting for news of a loved one who is thought to have been involved in a disaster. You learn to spot the helpers who come with the expectations of high levels of gratitude. They are often the same sort of people who will fill the silences with their own war stories or fail to recognise when a family needs to sit in quiet. Sometimes they are a little bit too curious about all the salacious details.

The bingo card of Bad Help

I keep a secret bingo card for the ways that we offer Bad Help to each other in everyday scenarios. One of the most common ways we don't help is by overpromising and then failing to deliver. Or maybe we'll be proud of ourselves for pushing a person in a wheelchair across the road without asking, when they greatly value their own autonomy. Or we start crowdfunding pages without checking whether it is what the recipient needs or wants. We might 'gift' help that actually requires the recipient to do more work than they are able at this time. Like activating subscriptions and uploading voucher card details, when somebody is physically and mentally frazzled.

Sometimes, attempts to help us when we're in a bad place can actually feel like dismissal. It's another moment when toxic positivity comes to the fore, often disastrously. We are fully programmed with all the platitudes and the unhelpful comparisons. Ready to go with 'he didn't suffer' or 'at least it was quick'. You can get another job, have another baby, try again. What about getting a rescue dog? These types of responses to our pain can, at times, seem that they are designed more for the other person to feel OK about our situation rather than for us, the person who is suffering. It's natural to want to make someone's pain go away, but trying to find 'solutions' to problems that simply cannot be solved can feel oppressive for the person in need.

Crucially, people need agency. Responders sometimes put in so many ways of supporting people that they take away all of their reasons to actually get up or keep going or think for themselves. They mean to be helpful by stripping away difficult choices or work, but when this goes on for months and years (food delivery, a person on hand as a taxi service, somebody to make calls or appointments) it actually makes the person less resilient, as – consciously or subconsciously – they no longer think they can do it for themselves.

I train what in the field of emergency response are called key workers or crisis support workers, who are there to support in the early days after disaster. Something we try to guard against is building in support that is there too long and strips away autonomy. Many times I have seen this leave people even more vulnerable, as when this is taken away, it renders them back at day one of the traumatic experience.

For the first few days after a sudden shock, people may need literally holding up. You may need to press food into their hands or remind them to lie down and sleep. But after about a week (which can be much earlier than may feel comfortable), allow them to help themselves and certainly try and get back outside and into a routine.

One of the most helpful things we can do is check our own responses to others in crisis and just take a little bit more time to think about what we will say. Dress rehearse it, even. All of us will encounter death, dying, sudden illness, baby loss, redundancy by proxy. It's worth putting the work in in advance. It might feel confronting, but we need to consider that offers of help can be performative and much more for the giver than the recipient.

All of this may sound alarming. As though by offering help you risk getting things wrong. And it's true that sometimes offering – and receiving – help takes a measure of courage. But luckily there is only one main thing to bear in mind. One guiding principle that can turn all help into Good Help.

The importance of dignity

As a child, I suffered from repeated kidney infections and was often admitted to hospital for further investigations. As I progressed into awkward puberty, these visits became more and more mortifying. Curtains would be pulled back as I was undressing or a bin would be emptied by a porter who was seemingly blind to the fact that I was being examined below the waist. The whiteboard by my bed would proclaim the nature of the problem and nurses would talk loudly about needing that urine sample from me – but they wouldn't use my name, they would talk about needing it from 'bed number three'. One time, I woke up feeling different to the examinations before and realised that they had examined much more of me than usual. Medical students bustled around the consultant and it was clear that they had examined me intimately while I was unconscious. This was common practice in medical training in the 1980s. The places where I was treated were teaching hospitals and conducting pelvic examinations on unconscious young girls was a teaching exercise until a few years ago.[22] I was devastated.

Everybody stood round me, in doctors' coats or scrubs, and were ostensibly there to help, to fix my body, but there was a blindness about what they might be doing to my soul and my spirit. They were there to help me and their training also meant they would go on to help many others. But they had tacked on a more selfish angle to the help that rendered it harmful. They used the moment to also suit their own needs – no different from somebody using a far-away tragedy to clear out a messy cupboard. Their 'help' took something from me.

As I write this chapter, I also have a tab open for a talk I am giving at a maternity conference about how lessons I have learned in disaster might be used in the care of new mothers in hospitals around the world. I ponder what links this to my vehemence around Bad Help, and my own experience, and the piles of dirty clothes clogging the runways after disaster, and my thoughts distil down to one word, one guiding tenet: dignity.

Dignity is a deep and complex philosophical concept, much more nuanced than may first appear. It's been over-simplistically explained as coming from the Latin word for 'worth' but actually, the Ancient Romans appear to have used it even more broadly. It seems inherently linked to a sense of self and to standing. To esteem and to self-determination.

It is the principle that probably guides me most in my work. To allow people the right to self-determine. To retain their own power. Not to humiliate them or belittle them. To not do further harm with my response. To act only with their full, informed consent.

The hardest type of advice for me to give to fellow responders has always been delivered into a hopeful face, a face desperate for you to tell them that they have done the 'right' thing. But it's not about winning a prize for doing good; it's about genuinely doing helpful things. One of the most important lessons I have learned is that several of the ways that we want to help each other when times are hard can actually do more harm.

Bad Help

And it is incredibly hard to call out because it is almost always coming from a good place, so it feels a bit like kicking a kitten.

One example is my constant crusade to protect the personal effects that will often be so important to families in incidents where the loved ones have died. Sometimes I get there too late and the Bad Help has already happened. Most often, in the last decade, the responders will have recovered them. Awareness has grown about the value of these items of clothing and toys and till receipts and hair clips and bottles of perfume. They place them into evidence bags and procure a local army barracks or industrial unit to store them.

But if I miss my moment the responders will have done more than I asked. The Bad Help will have crept in. They will have completed the first part of what I asked and carefully gathered up the items belonging to the deceased from the crash site. The shreds of fabric, the hoodies, the phone cases, the swimming goggles. But then they have done something else. Something I did not suggest. With the best of intentions. From a place of compassion. They have laundered the shirts, the blouses, the trousers with the floweriest fabric conditioner they could find. The responders desperately want me to be pleased. They show off their fabric piles like ladies in a 1960s department store. Sometimes there are even sheets of tissue paper and a ribbon.

They may even have overly censored the items, taking out anything they consider too ripped or dirty (thus robbing the families of that part of the story, if they want to learn it for themselves through touch and sight). Or even things that they consider not right to return – the condoms, the sex toys, and even recently I had a discussion about the returning of a cigarette lighter, not because it was unsafe, but because 'smoking is bad', as if this was some kind of exercise in subtle public health messaging within major tragedy.

This is a bad solution. It has stripped the dignity and the self-determination. The families of the dead are supposed to retain that one last chance, that one last choice and tiny bit of control. We have taken that from them too.

We need to ensure that dignity is built into everything we do.

Listening out

One of the truths that we found hard to talk about in 2020 was that in the years after pandemic, we were likely to see much greater instances of many types of illness. Lingering post viral infection. Delayed healthcare due to a creaking system. A clash of mental and physical illness as life just seemed to get harder. And as more people get ill, more people find themselves becoming carers. This likelihood was something that really stood out to me in the years before 2020 when the pandemic was something we just planned for on paper.

Over time, many people with chronic illness become expert at managing things like how to pace themselves. One of the greatest ways to offer Good Help is to understand what that might mean practically. If someone you care about needs to pace, which may mean missing events or opting out of things, lean into that. Help people to find the words to ask for what they need and to explain what works for them. Don't make it difficult or uncomfortable for them when they need to go home. Listen. Leave much longer gaps than feel comfortable to allow people to get past paralysing pride. Don't interrupt when they start to form the words that show they need help. Re-offer help and listening after three months and several times after. Don't be offended if it is turned down. 'Help' may be a triggering word in itself, linked to people feeling patronised or that their pride is dented. Often, it can also be taken as an implied criticism – 'do you need help in the garden?' can feel like 'I can see you have let the garden go'. So practise asking in a slightly different way and be receptive. Avoid offering fixes (manuka honey, shaman healers, an exorcism) unless you are asked specifically to source such things.

Practise asking for help yourself too. Hone skills of delegation and requesting support. Reframe seeking support as a strength and not in any way a weakness. One little test to flex those asking muscles is to try it for something small. Where the stakes are not too high. It's a good way to get past feelings like embarrassment and too much pride to ask for a lift or a cup of sugar.

Pay help forward but also allow others that you may have helped a lot over the years to pay something back to you. This can be small but the gesture is big. One of my dad's pupils once gave him a fun-size Mars Bar to say thank you for getting him through his craft design technology GCSE exam. The ratio of help: help didn't matter. The gesture was enough.

Once I have learned a new word, I tend to massively overuse it, and one that I apply so often to discussions of help is allyship. I am not looking for help, I am looking for an ally. Think of yourself as needing allies and expand your circle.

What does Good Help look like?

One of the greatest privileges of my work is the chance to see the times that the good help works. The time I was able to return the personal effects at the right time, and watch a smile spread across the fiancée's face as she opened the small cardboard box and then held the wallet to her cheek. She actively looked for the scuff on its leather that I stopped someone buffing out. It was there before and was a happy reminder of a week on a Greek Island. She traced it with her forefinger. 'He damaged the wallet scrambling to get from the boat to the jetty the night he proposed,' she told me.

I have learned that the personal effects gathered at the scene, safely stored, can wait a few days. The talk about the funeral can also wait. In less-life-changing scenarios I have learned that often the evenings are better for quiet, reflective non-verbal help – pushing a piece of fruit cake into a worrying hand or suggesting a walk in the twilight. More active talks about things that might help are better in the morning. A lot of the guidance about 'disaster recovery' comes down to pacing and to timing. That is true at home too.

How to help in bereavement is something we will all need to do and to get better at. I think about the time when my mum's friend – also widowed, with her own experience of what was needed – called round with some fairy lights to soften the blow of widow grief that comes when summer turns to autumn and the person you love is still dead but it's now dark. And they made my mum chuckle with delight, briefly.

When my dad died, I was very aware from my work that other people find grieving people very difficult and messy to be around. So I made a pact early on with Mum that I would try my best to just be there to listen, and I would not be embarrassed or try to stop her crying. Mum says that one of her biggest revelations has been to reflect awkwardly on all the times she might have dropped a clanger over the years, now that she too is bereaved. So try to actively train out of yourself phrases like 'everything happens for a reason' or 'he is in a better place'. Ask somebody 'how are you *today*?' rather than the expansive 'how are you?' Never be afraid to say the name of the person in conversation. Be brave by leaning into the difficult things that you are not sure the person wants to talk about. Ask someone if they are alright, and then ask again.

Get a little braver in your help. This can mean not using a euphemism and not skirting around the person or subject. We avoid things too long in conversation because we are afraid. But one thing my work has really hammered home is that we must lose that fear. No matter how hard we find it to talk to someone about what happened to them, we must always remember it's harder for them and now is the time to be braver.

Never underestimate tiny help. A hand on an arm, human touch, not crossing the road when we see a bereaved friend because we are embarrassed. A cup of tea (this is the key to most of my lessons). A card or a text message. Delayed help is also good. In my own family and friends' situations, I often send initial messages of support and then back off. I wait for them to tell me that the casseroles and lasagnes have stopped arriving. The need for help will be infinite. You can be there when they are ready for you, when the honeymoon phase has faded away.

My dad had a particular approach to delivering help, which when he died, we included in the eulogy. He had a rare way of making the recipient feel touched by a warmth that was without any condescension or even the tiniest dint to pride. Like you were actually doing him a gentle favour. The experience of receiving the help from him was entirely painless. There was no ego or mansplaining.

The physical manifestation of this is 'Dad's souk' – a garage he built himself that is filled from bottom to top with things that somebody may need and that would be given away freely and constantly. There is rope and pliers and spare kettles and a hundred spanners. A shopping trolley. He just liked helping and he did it so well and he expected nothing from it. He had a way of maintaining the recipient's dignity, so special and so noticeable, that this quality featured in just about every letter and card that we received after his death. The best way to describe it is by borrowing a little from Rudyard Kipling's 'The Land'.[23] It's a poem about ownership and working of the fields, and a poacher who has an innate knowledge of the land he works. When offering advice, the wise older poacher would offer it gently – 'Hev it jest as you've a *mind* to, but, if I was you, I'd . . .'

Dad would think long and hard about how to explain the message, to pass on the thing that just perfectly met the need; how to help the hearer of the message to feel empowered and able to complete the project or walk a bit taller. He was careful to never squash anyone's enthusiasm. And it was such a potent quality that it seems to have lingered on. If I stay quiet just long enough and ask him for help, from somewhere, he is still ready with an 'If I was you, I might . . .'

Your recovery kit

Be very intentional when you offer help.
You are very likely to be overpromising. Women are particularly bad at this. Be brutally realistic about the time you actually have available to help. Studies have shown that when women are asked to add up the tasks they have planned as units of time, they often come to thirty to forty hours when they only have *a five or six hour window*. In all training that we do in emergency response, we emphasise that being specific is very important.

No woolly offerings. Set a time to come round and do what you said you would do.

Feed thy neighbours.
Drop in teabags and biscuits. Everybody I have ever asked who has walked through times of crises remembers and values the food that was dropped in. Always try to take homemade items in plastic containers or on a plate that you don't mind not getting back. One of my common experiences is a family, in the midst of loss, being mithered for that missing plate.

Remember that donations of goods are the secondary disaster.
Since the pandemic years, I have been working with the National Emergencies Trust on an initiative to get the message out to give money rather than physical donations. The hashtag is #CashNotStuff. This advice works best in advance so work with your school or mosque or business to channel it loud, before any event, and provide explanations as to why. It makes a great assembly presentation. There may be occasions when there are very specific requests for 'stuff' so a local hospital will ask for mobility aids or a charity will ask for your spare spectacles. But generally, the rule of thumb is always to donate money instead.

Lesson Six
Hopium

It can be the hope that kills you. In New Orleans, in August 2005, as responders took stock of the devastation caused by Hurricane Katrina, they left a trail of spray-painted messages on the houses for those who followed them. When the rescuers found somebody had died in the roof space, they would paint a code to indicate a body, or, more starkly, simply write '1 dead in attic'. The paint would be there until the house was rebuilt or demolished. The death toll spelled out in spray paint included many elderly men and women who had hoped to wait out the consequences of Katrina in the same way they had decades of earlier hurricanes that had battered Louisiana. They took to their attics with a bedspread and a bottle of juice. And with hope.

TV shows and the writers of thrillers make much of the stories that a crime scene tells of what happened there. Clues to the killer, hints of a violent back story. But the clues that I see most frequently written into the scene of disaster by those who died is hope. Hope of rescue. Hope that help is coming over the hill. Hope that the storm will be less severe than the forecasters predicted. Hope that things will get better. Except that sometimes it isn't hope. It's something far more tempting and slippery and dangerous: what I call *hopium*.

One day in late August 2005, while we were working on the aftermath of the 7 July attacks on the London tube network, my fellow emergency planners and I turned on the TV to watch the news, our attention caught by the weather forecast for the southern states of America. The USA was considered by British emergency planners to be an emergency planning superpower, and we would furiously try to copy and paste their ideas. I had seen the hidden challenges, the reality of some aspects of the response to 9/11 myself, but even I had bought into the idea of their readiness and their power. Conferences in the early 2000s extolled 'Do It the American Way' as everyone clamoured to have Rudy Giuliani, then mayor of New York, open their English emergency planning event. It never occurred to us that when it came to their next disaster, help might not come. We watched the Americas and the Caribbean respond to hurricanes every year. Maybe we had become a little blasé. They certainly had. This was just another big 'un, but eminently handleable.

And then the New Orleanians started to drown.

Hurricane Katrina was fierce. She tore across the northern Gulf Coast, 125-mile-per-hour winds tearing at roofs and trees. But then she colluded with a manmade deficiency and errors in design and something truly terrible was unleashed.

There are no natural disasters. There are Mother-Earth initiated events (and wow, is she peeved at the moment) that begin deep within the Earth's core or atmosphere, but as soon as they hit a community or a structure they become entangled with human error and deficiencies. Humans are always in there somewhere. This time, in New Orleans, the levees and flood walls, designed to protect the residents from catastrophe, failed. They simply could not withstand the force. There were a number of other factors that compounded to make the tragedy truly manmade, including the terrifying levels of poverty that had been inflicted on local residents in the years before the disaster.

Eighty per cent of New Orleans was flooded in a few hours, and one parish, St Bernard Parish, was lost completely. Like so many disasters, the death toll remains contested and has recently been revised to 1,392 people. Around 134,000 homes were affected and the National Centers for Environmental Information estimate the cost at $190 billion.

Many of the older residents of New Orleans had experienced multiple weather events and had particular memories of surviving Hurricane Betsy in 1965. She too had wreaked havoc across the United States Gulf Coast but had left some residents with a strong evidence base for their hope. Betsy had done her worst but they had survived. Earlier, similar events, reframed as survivable near-misses, can often lead to a fatal bias that 'we've got this'.

This time, the sheer force of the winds and rain also disabled most of the communications systems that responders rely upon at both state and national level. The help that we expected to see, the sort that's in the movies, simply did not come.

Hope or hopium?

Hope and hopium, twin actors, can play out simultaneously in so many situations. One is constructive, useful, the thing that may just, if we are lucky, bring us safely to shore. The other is deadening and dangerous. Hopium fills the ears with cloth. It is ultimately perhaps best described as an over-estimation of the positives of a situation. It makes us hold on to something for too long before the crushing realisation comes that the hope was always fragile. I think of hopium as an over-reliance on hope and an inability to temper it.

In disaster, hope and hopium are invariably there, often from even before the moment of impact, through the initial response and pervading the grand plans for a smooth recovery. It is also one of the causes of clashes amongst neighbourhoods and survivors on what to do next. The challenge – perhaps now, more than ever – is to distinguish between the two.

Like most people, I have a tormented relationship with hope. Of course I want to believe in it, and of course disaster planners have their own special ways of working with it. It's even right there in my surname. When do we decide to hold on to it and how can we make the best use of it? And equally, how can we tell when hope has turned toxic and stultifying? What is the difference between real, constructive hope and the false friend of hopium? Psychologists have also begun to explore whether staying optimistic about a situation may provide a boost to our personal resilience, particularly if there is a long road ahead.

One group of people who greatly influenced how I think about this were the women of the village of Toll Bar, Doncaster. This is a place that has flooded repeatedly and also has endured multiple other batterings. It was profoundly affected by the closure of local mines and then later by austerity and political neglect. In empirical studies, it is shown to have high levels of poverty and deprivation – but is simultaneously one of the most inspiring places I have seen. The women I met there have been a source of life wisdom and collective experience that I use on a daily basis. I got to know them at a community room in a primary school, hearing their stories of life after flooding. But often we ended up talking about so much more. They knew a lot about the difference between hope and hopium. Knowing that difference might sometimes have saved their lives.

Some of these women had stayed in abusive relationships because maybe he would change and tomorrow would be a better day. But eventually, hope had been revealed for what it was, hopium, and they had managed to escape. Sometimes – when all the warning signs were being minimised, by love and longing and fear of abandonment – this realisation would require incredibly tough words from those around them. Others had been evicted from their first proper home because they had believed that a miracle would come as the bills and eviction notices had stacked up. Hopium also played its part in times when they had been scammed or stolen from.

As older women, they were now furious that hopium had taken from them some of the best years of their lives and were quick with advice for younger women who were giving their partner one more chance or holding out for a terrible boss to leave. And that's one of the cruellest things about believing in hopium. It robs you of precious time. That might be the time needed to evacuate in a hurricane or years of your life believing in a new beginning that isn't coming unless you make a major change.

One of the most difficult moments in a disaster aftermath is that point at which people realise that belief in those around them, in institutions and systems to act justly and safely, might have been hopium too. As a former mining community, the women of Toll Bar knew this well. I worry about this a lot when I am evaluating plans for our chemical, power and nuclear factories. How will both the employees and the local community (many of whom are also employees) feel if something goes wrong? If an employer that generations of families have relied on were to kill and harm? In Gresford, as in so many places after disaster, this coalesced into disbelief and rage. The realisation that their bosses did not have their backs was made clear on day one when the surviving men's wages were docked for not finishing *that* shift.

I'm not advocating the dark cynicism of 'trust no one' but there has to be realism and pragmatism in there too. One of the truisms that rattled alongside our emergency planning for a future pandemic in the early 2000s was just how changed the world would be. We knew people would inevitably ask a lot more and trust a lot less. All disaster survivors do. Organisations would have to work harder than ever to ensure they were reaching out to people and getting communication methods right. They had a responsibility to watch out for encouraging hopium and had to take their role as a trusted source seriously. What this meant for hope was actually quite positive. People would probably want a lot more detail and an evidence base, there would be a lot less blind following.

When hope is necessary

The women of Toll Bar had also stayed hopeful for other things. One woman had suffered eighteen baby losses, something that resonated with me on a very personal level. It was actually how I really got to know the women, as they ferreted out my own issues with fertility, recognising the grey face and the frequent visits to their loo while ostensibly there to learn more about floods. Many of them also knew the kind of hopium-laced advice women get in these circumstances from friends, family and the medical profession: *it is simply one of those things. It happens to a quarter of all women. Just go again.* In my soul, I knew this was false advice, though coming generally from a good and compassionate place. It was also advice that suited the medical profession and stopped them from being bombarded by worried women.

Hope and hopium are completely entangled in a person's journey to having children. How to differentiate? One thing I have applied in my own life and when gently talking to friends is to try to look at the situation as objectively as possible. How much of a toll is it taking on me and my relationship? What if I took the thing I was hopeful for and removed it completely? Took it off the table?

I am now lucky enough to have two daughters – Elizabeth was going to be my last throw of the dice; Mabel truly is a miracle. I sought advice from clinicians that I had built a good dialogue with and asked them if I needed to give up, and they replied 'you are not there yet'. Because they knew that not all of life is mapped. Miracles do happen. And they happened for this woman, with eighteen losses, as well as for me – for both of us, two daughters appeared. The only way that you can stay believing that one day you will be a mum in those circumstances, and sign up to the same draining experiences over and over again, is via an infusion of pure and necessary hope.

Hopium and our future

Hopium rears its head often in discussions of how to respond to and live alongside a rapidly changing climate. We are mired in a chronic crisis – not just climatically, but ideologically, in terms of how to think about it. We need to know when to stay hopeful and when to start getting busy.

For a myriad of reasons, the world's weather is changing. Sea levels will rise, many places will be under water in a century. Faced with an inhospitable environment, humans will do what we have been doing throughout history: we will have to move, and on a scale never seen before. This is not a future problem. This is a now problem.

One of the first coastal towns in the United Kingdom that will be the very reluctant poster child for a forced migration is up the road from me. Renowned for its beach and its miniature railway built in 1895, the beautiful Welsh town of Fairbourne has been defined brutally by policy makers as 'unsustainable'.

As is the UK way, our starting point for chronic emergency is usually a series of dry, jargon-heavy engineering reports.

The engineers have declared that Fairbourne will be below normal high tide levels within the next fifty years. There are also high groundwater levels and a high risk of surface water flooding in the village. The villagers will need to relocate. This has naturally led to turmoil in this small place with its shops and cafes, little railway and hundreds of houses.

House prices plummeted for a time but, interestingly, there was also an influx of new residents who stated that they were determined to enjoy this beautiful place, nestled in front of the Eryri national park, while it is still here. Refusing to let the future be written yet and enjoying life in the right now.

But Fairbourne is a portent. This decision about whether somewhere is too unsafe to return to will have to be made over and over again in the next century. I am already seeing it (and it's a problem playing out globally). There is a new conversation being added to recovery after flooding. Now, *sotto voce*, I hear: *there may be no going back to this place*. Or, more brutally, somebody has run the figures and its simply not worth rebuilding somewhere that may be gone in the next thirty years. Residents may not be able to go home or if they do, they will be flooded out again.

For centuries, humans have lived in places that flood, but now that risk is so likely that anything other than complete resettlement is too unsafe. They are now so eroded that it may simply not be safe to rehome people there. This 'managed retreat' that has been a theme of climate conferences for decades has now come home to roost. This began as a growing issue for coastal towns but is now becoming a regular feature of my aftermath discussions after all sorts of flood events. The responders want a way to warn the residents about what the future may hold but they don't know how to go there.

Maybe there is no going home again for people who live alongside rivers and gorges too. In the UK, it is raining harder and for longer than it ever has before. We are experiencing more and more extreme weather events and we are simply not ready for them. And the planners, scientists and engineers generally haven't found the right way to say it.

At some of the meetings I have been having recently about 'managed retreat' – talking candidly to communities about not being able to return home – I have been surprised at how casually some colleagues think it can be done. When they start to write their plans for shifting whole communities out of their homes and their lifescapes, they strip out any sense of feeling or sentiment. They write business plans and project flow charts but have no time for the work that needs to be done to support people going through this. There is also little thought given to how we get through whatever comes next. They have forgotten that it is not just about topography and structures – it's about people and the heart within them. I understand their need to crush the hopium but there is a need to retain the hope. That a future, and a good one, is still possible.

When it comes to climate change issues, it is hopium to think 'it will all be fine', but it is also way too depressing to say there is nothing that can be done about the big issues. I have a resistance to hopium but I feel equal concern about doom-mongering. I hold the hope in one hand and behave with practicality alongside it. A lifetime of this work has shown me that individuals and communities are usually pretty resilient.

Positive changes

Our ambivalence to hope is captured in a phrase that emergency planners use a lot – the 'reasonable worst-case scenario'. The first word reflects a pragmatism, a willingness to listen and maybe the idea that there is still some hope. The other words are there to try to spell things out. It is time to be much more realistic and much more comfortable with the reasonable worst-case scenario. We need to talk more about living alongside a changing climate, rather than assuming we will be able to change the trajectory. The difference between hope and hopium is crucial here. Hopium blights our attitudes and colours our vision. It is anti-evidence and numbing. It allows us to be passive, to think disaster won't happen – that if it does, we can do enough to spot it and avert it. Hope is different – it tells us ways to improve things and live alongside disaster effectively.

On the other hand, leaning too far into the doom ('what's the point when all the icecaps are going to melt?') can lead to a kind of nihilism, giving a general state-of-the-world depression a set of legitimising scaffolding that is unhelpful. It can be strangely comforting to think of yourself as pretty meaningless or small in the scheme of things, but my work has taught me that nothing could be further from the truth. Just because things are uncertain does not mean that they are hope*less*. And just because the task ahead is huge does not mean your contribution is not vital.

I see the way that people change the world all the time – laws get altered or amended. New guidance is issued. A garden is planted. A child is given a fresh start.

I am working on this chapter after spending a day with a delegation of Korean families, who are survivors and the bereaved from ten recent disasters. A new centre for disaster rights has flown them over to learn from the UK way of doing things. It is very early days in the slump for some of them. They ask me what is the thing that keeps me hopeful, keeps me going, and I tax my translator by waxing lyrical about all of the differences and changes that I see in my work. All the way that people come together. The researchers call it 'pro-social' – people working together do great things. They must watch out for hopium but equally avoid the loss of all hope – the translator types furiously into her online tool for that one!

Five bad winters

In our own lives, the difference between hope and hopium often comes down to the facts sitting behind them. An important part of differentiating between the two depends on what we are listening to and the evidence we are being given. This became painfully clear in the pandemic with the notion that the disruption or extreme control measures 'might last six weeks'. That was beyond even hopium. It was disaster wishful thinking on a scale I had never seen before.

This was a particularly lonely time for me as some of the country's most senior leaders, journalists, broadcasters and politicians parroted this hopium that went against the experience of any previous epidemic. It was contrary to every evidence base I had ever seen. I knew that the disruption would be immense and I took to measuring it like an old farmer as 'at least five bad winters'. In the summer of 2020, I was asked if I would appear on an evening magazine TV show to talk about 'what might come next'. After I outlined to the researcher my thoughts that the acute disruption would last for years before segueing into a slump that would feel viscous and miserable, the producers, for understandable reasons, dropped the segment.

I still don't quite know how we should have approached this – people tell me that it would have been helpful to know a little more about what would come in the pandemic aftermath. The strains on an already bashed healthcare system, excess deaths, geopolitical tensions, a general feeling of 'meh' that infiltrates all areas of our lives. And my work has drilled into me that realism and honesty are always better in the long term. But I do hear the people who say that in order to stop people giving up, we had to temper the messages.

What I can say is that one of the hardest things to see has been the looks of horror on people's faces when they realise we held something back. And this is definitely something we always need to take into account in our own lives. Understanding the differences between hope and hopium is an important lesson for people who often deliver important, life-changing messages, like lawyers and clinicians. There is a particular obligation on them to understand the implications of allowing people to buy into an easy-to-deliver hopium.

Hopium is very closely linked to denial. Denial is a very powerful and defensive emotion: it prevents us from taking stock and stops us from conducting the impact assessment we know we need. Though a little bit of denial allows us to buy some necessary time to get well or take some space to not worry for once. We don't have a right to grab somebody by the lapels, shake them and demand that they leave their denial behind. It may be providing a brief and protective space for healing. But generally, and particularly when it becomes a state of being rather than a temporary moment of reprieve, denial is deeply harmful.

I have learned a lot in this area from those who work in end-of-life care. They have provided very useful advice on how to give relatively realistic messages about the pathway of someone's illness. This demands a careful tempering of any cruelty and bluntness, an acknowledgement that not all is known and the gentlest extraction of hopium. The real hope no longer comes from the thought of a long life but the potential of a good death with ends tied up.

The potency of denial-induced hopium is most often demonstrated when it comes to illness. 'They are clinging on to hope,' we say to each other sagely, in the face of some terrible disease. Is there a more nuanced balance to be struck? Do we ask enough about what will really happen? What time with our loved one, or answers to questions, is this hopium robbing from us?

I see denial in my own family all the time, particularly relating to illness and ageing, and it does of course require a delicate approach. It is not for me to shout through a loudhailer that they are kidding themselves.

But I do take kin who are putting themselves at great risk by not making any care plans at all by the hand to say, 'I don't think this situation will get any better.' The other relatives will often look horrified. This was not the bargain – the pact is we tell each other that things will be fine and my words had broken some hidden sisterhood rule. But then I watched the ill person do something that I also see in disaster-affected communities all the time. Physically grow, sitting straighter in front of me. Breathing in, deep within the ribcage, and very slowly starting to form the first steps of a plan.

In our own lives, hopium may leave us stultified, paralysed and unable to think. It may see us placing too much trust in the idea that help is coming. It may cause us to forget or relinquish our own power and our own agency. It may leave us highly vulnerable to empty promises of happy endings and get-rich-quick schemes.

Hopium is sold as something that is fast; hope can often take much longer. As Rebecca Solnit reminds us in her writing about hope, it took women three quarters of a century to get the vote. But some things are definitely worth the long game.

Edges of hopefulness

Too much hopium gets in the way of being receptive to clear advice that something has gone or is about to go wrong. But if you can imagine that things go wrong, you may be able to do something about it. Emergency planners are very wary of hopium. We urge our colleagues to go further, darker, in their thinking. We interrogate those who come to us with hope in their plans to turn their analysis on its head and work with us, just for a minute, on what happens if the good things don't materialise. If something looks too good to be true it often is. We sense-check our hope with each other. And we don't shoot the non-hopeful messenger if they try to bring some necessary cynicism to the discussions.

Sometimes you might be using hopium as a slightly lazy way to bring a difficult conversation to an end – 'I am sure it will be fine.' Or incubating hopium by reinforcing a level of denial or enabling a harmful behaviour.

Work with the Reasonable Worst-Case Scenario in your own life. I think most emergency planners bring this home. We expect and plan for things like upheaval in our employment or for sudden illness. We keep a weather eye on the things around us in the world and in our immediate eyeline. A friend once told me off for looking away from him at a party; he said I was showing disinterest in the story he was telling. I wasn't but I had spotted the early signs of an altercation between a man and a woman over by the staircase. It was escalating fast. Emergency planners get our lumps checked and attend our health screenings. We watch the emergency exits and the mood changes in a room.

If you live with slightly more expectation of a more serious scenario emerging you can also hone your startle factor. I don't get it right all the time but there are ways that living readier helps you to manage that initial set of reactions at the start of bad news. Thinking worst-case scenario allows you to work through some likely scenarios and what actions you might need to go with them. Having this in hand is surprisingly beneficial for you and those around you. The key to managing down your startle factor is to remember that calm can be contagious. As Jolie and Elizabeth say in their 'Calamity Cards', calm can be as contagious as stress or anxiety. Sounding calm can also be practised. It is one of the most important skills to hone and can make a profound difference to other people in distress and to children. The first time that I took 'the call' – a need for a full mass fatality response – it was for a plane crash over a southern German town. I remember marvelling at the calm tone in the man's voice as he told me about the mid-air carnage. He had lowered his tone, slowed his speech and knew that the most important thing was to make sure that I had all the information I needed. Clearly. This meant working against a whole host of bodily reactions that would prickle his skin and make his speech rapid and squeaky. That moment has guided me ever since. Airlines rehearse frequently and I wondered if the calmness was the result of the regular practice or a coping strategy learned elsewhere. We see it in control room operators for the emergency services and in healthcare workers and lawyers. But it's a skill and has to be taught and honed. As well as my calm voice I also have my 'shouty' but controlled voice for when you really need to be heard, such as in a first aid situation. Work on yours.

Get as much information as you can. Read slow things slowly – the news cycle does not lend itself to staying hopeful, but instead try to read books and evidenced articles. I try to have at least one 'look at this wonderful tale of hope/look at this beating of the odds' in every five articles that I read. But also leave a little bit of room for the acceptance that hopefulness actually goes hand in hand with uncertainty. I can't tell you it will be OK, but you can be OK with that.

Hope is not for the impatient. Watching the hope seedlings grow takes years. Decades even. Its outcomes are not predictable – and that frustrates the recoverers and the management consultants. It also has an extra kicker of frustration because we may not be the ones to see the fruit. There are years in between when it can seem like all hope is lost and the eventual successful rebuilding. The children and grandchildren of the Gresford miners are grandparents now. They will never see the full power of the build and the effect of thousands of tiny little hopeful changes.

But I have seen what hope does and fuels more than most people. I have seen that the possibilities are near-endless. I get to see, in my work, the drawing of a cathedral become an actual cathedral. I get to see the children of a destroyed place sketch out their dream ice cream parlour. And then when I go back it has become an actual ice cream parlour. I get to see the manifest become the reality. Friends who I have rocked as they mourned a lost partner find new, different but good, love again. My beloved friends Sue and Mike on their wedding day, held just as soon as she could walk down the aisle again after losing her leg on an underground train on 7 July 2005.

In the end, I am never going to be talked out of the importance of holding on to the right kind of hope because without it, what is the point? Real hope propels us. It puts energy through our feet and up into my veins. It brought us our daughters. Hope is a warrior emotion.[24] It involves action and bravery and willingness to walk a little ahead of everyone else. Every day, hope powers us to get something future, something ethereal done. How do you know the difference between the two? That's the trick. Real hope is harnessed to work and energy and bravery and propulsion. Check yourself – does this hope feel rebellious[25] and radical and pessimistically optimistic and risky? Only then do we know it's the real deal.

Your recovery kit

Manifest.

It's not just for movie stars! As well as thinking about worst-case things I am also a big believer in dream – believe – achieve. There are limits on this of course (I am never going to dance with the Royal Ballet!). But I am often shocked at the limits people put on themselves. With the dreams of family, we tend to start with a bit of research on what might be possible, how will we undertake and resource it, what support will we need and a back-up plan. We seek external advice on whether we are fuelled by hopium (do we have the talent or skills necessary – back to the ballet point) and we check in regularly on whether the plan is working.

Think about evacuation.
Or even just about how you will handle a call with difficult news. In the next few years, we know we are likely to see more sudden cuts to our power and water, either from issues like weather or an infrastructure problem or because of cyber issues. We will almost all see sudden illness or rushes to hospital. Discuss out loud (that's really all a plan is) with your household and people who may depend on you. Please think about your pets too: the RSPCA has advice on their website for a pet emergency plan.

Stay very alert for scamming and fraud.
One of the first conversations I have in the hours after something like a weather emergency or flooding is with trading standards about what new scams are circulating. No area innovates faster than the sorts of frauds that trade on hopium.

Find 'trusted' sources for good quality information.
Trust in science, medicine, weather information and just about everything else has taken a big hit in recent years. I feel a responsibility on social media to signpost accurately and even the best organisations

get it wrong sometimes, so this is not straightforward but generally, my go-tos are local news, local councils and the Met Office for local emergency planning news. Emergency planning philosophy is if there are conflicting views – one more severe than the other – plan for the worst one and if we 'overreact' that's better than not being ready.

We are all going to die.
Any other belief is hopium. It is worth it for your family to spend time on lasting powers of attorney, wills and arrangements for your children. If we are lucky, we might also get old and that is worth planning for too.

Learn how to say no.
Don't be the cause of somebody else's misplaced hopium. I am a people-pleaser and when I was younger, I was rightly called out for letting people think I might make it to an event (encouraging hopium), when in fact I just did not know how to say no. 'No' really is a complete sentence and requires no further explanation. I note down phrases that people use to bring something to a respectful end like, 'I won't be there but I want you to have a great night.' Or, 'That's not something I want to do.' The other person's disappointment is not for you to fix.

See hope as a rebellious, doing emotion.
It is something you are choosing to do rather than

going blindly along with. Try to think of one thing every day that you feel hopeful about. I choose to be very hopeful about the strength and the wisdom and the new ways of thinking that are present in the generations after me.

Lesson Seven
Holding Two Truths

The birth of my first living baby girl was a hot mess of blue lights and blood transfusions and me politely asking if I was going to die. There was emergency surgery and a spell in a high dependency unit. Afterwards, I asked for a meeting to explore this experience, but what quickly became apparent was that the clinicians in the room fervently believed their own version of events. This was not just slight differences of perspective or even legally advised defensiveness; I realised they were adamant that what I remembered simply could not have happened. There was nothing I could say to change that. The only way to arbitrate through that would be to escalate further and further up a complaints process, which seemed so far away from my original aim of a positive conversation. One where together we would identify some simple improvements that could be made.

This brought very close to home what a lifetime of work in disaster had already taught me: in moments of trauma, people see events very differently, and that their conditioning and their biases will fix these 'truths' in their minds like a fly caught in amber. They will also often take their version of events to the grave, regardless of the amount of truth and reconciliation processes thrust upon them.

Even two people looking out of the same window at the same situation unfolding remember different things. It's like that optical illusion you sometimes find circulating on the internet – is it a rabbit or a duck that you see in the picture? Then there are the lenses and biases given to us by our upbringings and even the different ways that our brains work to take into account. Memories are shaped differently for different people. And sometimes people deliberately forget or have their recollections changed for them. There are darker deceptions too; coached lying and deliberate deception.

There are times when we may be reluctant to open ourselves up to other truths because they are linked to feelings that fester within us, such as pride, disappointment or deep hurt. We need the other person to be solely at fault. We see this in a lot of social and personal interactions. How we remember our childhoods, how friendships played out and particularly in relationship breakdowns. The latter often involves navigating a path where two or more parties have completely different recollections of series of events.

Teachers and parents are constant arbiters of young children's struggles with two truths. Little shoulders heave at the unfairness of an adult deciding what happened to cause the spilled juice or playground argument. I remember that feeling well, but now that I am an adult, I realise that sometimes it may not always be important that your memory is the winner. But there are times when it does matter. The challenge for us all is to discover when those times might be and to fight for them. People will often stay mired in the slump having unwinnable fights. Locked in battles with wraiths that cannot be fully grasped. Some truths will always elude, while at other times, explanations need to be quarried.

Balancing truths

The first time I saw somebody deftly and delicately balance multiple truths, I had been sitting for hours in the back of a court in Blackburn watching my Uncle Mike. I was a teenager doing work experience. He was a coroner, a senior judge whose role in cases of sudden and unexpected death is to establish in a court room who somebody was and how, where and when they died. We can pretend all we like that evidence or forensics can complete the jigsaw, but ultimately there are always lacunas in memory or gaps in the known facts. The coroner is a societally appointed arbiter whose job is to tie up all the complicated threads into a neater package.

That there can be multiple truths is brought to the fore whenever a young person appears to have brought about their own death using pills, cutting or a ligature. There are always many, many stories and reasons why they might have arrived at this point. Sometimes, there might be a note and clear evidence of pre-planning. But, even then, there are almost always many inconsistencies or challenges. When something like a lethal amount of medication is involved, there might be a very fine line between an accident and a deliberate act. In these situations, and in many others, can a coroner, who had never met the child, really determine one clear version of the truth?

I think it was in those wood-panelled rooms that I learned the most about the truth juggling that is essential for some aspects of life. In deaths as a result of suicide, Uncle Mike would sometimes give a narrative verdict – a legally approved story that allows the multiple truths to sit together – rather than coming down hard on one sieved and concentrated version. This takes the form of a longer verdict that can hold the multiple truths in one document where the story is recorded, including the contradictions and complexities. The narrative verdict respects the only real truth – which is that sometimes we simply cannot know everything entirely.

However, this approach has its potential pitfalls too. In January 2017, Colin Pritchard, a psychiatric social worker and social researcher at Bournemouth University, published research that suggested coroners were 'under-reporting' suicide in England and Wales by up to 50 per cent through leaning towards 'gentler' verdicts such as accidental death or a narrative verdict. The narrative approach works well as a way of holding multiple different accounts but was potentially obscuring the real level of loss.

According to official statistics, 6,188 people ended their own lives in the UK in 2015, up from 6,122 in

2014. But Pritchard said a more accurate estimate was in fact 9,000. He stated that the true number of teenage suicides could be as high as 270, rather than the 186 recorded by the government, but that this was hidden by coroners in an attempt to comfort grief-stricken families who would prefer to believe the death was an accident.

It is right that society understands its responsibilities to these young people, but I also felt the burden on the shoulders of individual coroners. One partial solution was to change the standard of proof. This – the level of evidence needed by coroners to conclude whether a death was caused by suicide – was changed from the criminal standard of 'beyond all reasonable doubt' to the civil standard of 'on the balance of probabilities' on 26 July 2018. Deaths recorded as suicides increased. But what I learned in that court room in Lancashire has stayed with me: how hard it can be to be definitive – to distil everything down to one overriding truth – when human frailties and complexities are at stake.

Bad news and kindness

I see distillation to one narrative almost daily in my work. I see responders leaning into a gentler but neatened and problematic story – 'she did not suffer'; 'they were sleeping when it happened' – only for a muddier, complex, but much more likely sounding bundle of truths to start to emerge later. Truth and trust are inextricably linked, and I see many families lose all faith in the system when they realise that sympathetic platitudes have crossed over into falsehood. As emergency responders, we find that we simply don't always know how to tell the truth, but that is a skill that can be worked on. I always urge response colleagues to look again at whether they are using 'two faces'. This is where we tell the survivors and bereaved a banal, softly lit version of the events and save the more candid, complicated, more accurate version for behind closed doors. Sometimes I still see bare-faced lies or collusions often repackaged as 'necessary for operational reasons'. I call those the 'toxic nuggets' – the harmful lies that we may have to live with until a brave whistleblower or investigative journalist unearths them.

There is a growing body of work that has produced training for everyone, from students of medicine and palliative care to geologists and veterinarians, on how to break bad news truthfully. It considers everything from language used to the setting in which the discussion happens. Platitudes and euphemisms do harm. Instead, what you are aiming for is complete honesty, delivered with compassion and in amounts that people can deal with. Try to think like a good, well-trained police family liaison officer. Package the truth with gentleness and in manageable chunks. In my work, we provide some written information in case the other person does not take in what we are telling them. It's possible to practise truthful delivery of bad news in easier situations. We all use 'white lies' far more than we realise.

This is where I am heartened most by what came after us. My generation grew up telling everyone that everything was OK and using white lies like tissue. But I have noted with great relief that often, Generation Z has a very different relationship with the two faces. They tend to speak with a candour and a disarming clarity that has been missing in much of my career. I do everything I can to protect that in meetings. They hold their truth. I hope it stays that way.

There are times when the truths can be held all together and times when it probably does not matter whether it is a duck or a rabbit. After disasters, there are usually not just two or three truths, but tens of truths. Some of them simply cannot be true together. One thing I have learned is how to operate alongside that. When it's a conflict between survivors' and the bereaved's versions of events with that of responders, then there is a new etiquette often of just allowing those many truths to just be. This is easier to do if the multiple versions of a truth seem lighter and less painful.

Some years ago, after one severe flood, there was a 'community truth' – a rapidly spreading story in the evacuation centres – that Queen Elizabeth II was due to visit. This then really took on legs and became the story that the Queen was visiting and, rather surreally, would also be gifting every household a full set of bath towels. As far as I know from responders, the Queen was never expected to visit, and certainly not with any bath towels. But some flood survivors remained adamant and were deeply disappointed. I heard the story of the Regal slight several times and to correct or challenge it seemed unnecessary or cruel.

Mining for truths

We live in a world, particularly since the advent of social media, which really struggles with taking time over truth seeking. We have also become more tribal. Holding one view only gives us keys to the club. While this is a seductive way of thinking, it is dangerous because it is polarising, and it prevents us from understanding in our hearts that every event can be seen from multiple viewpoints.

Straight out of university, I went to intern with Katy Jones, a senior television producer. I was set to work on a production about the events of Bloody Sunday in 1972. Katy's approach to investigative research was absolutely rigorous. She took things in her stride, such as the fact that her phone had clearly been tapped. And that our office post would arrive opened and in transparent Royal Mail bags with no further explanation. This wasn't the first time this had happened to her and she saw it as a sign she was onto something good. Her life's work was burrowing underneath the state-approved view of the story.

As with all good interviewers, Katy let the person go wherever they wanted as they told their story and I would explore the transcripts with her later for things that would work on camera. I was tasked with fact checking the material that related to the events on that fateful Sunday and particularly the weeks before. Mapping and plotting locations. It was important to find all the versions of the truths in painstaking detail about the hours leading up to the shootings. Katy was desperate to ensure that they could evidence where people had been. It was a crucial and early introduction to the documents, chronologies and timelines that, when put together, pulse with an urgency that something foretold and clear to see was about to happen.

Working in investigative research, of the highest quality, taught me something that has endured as a vital lesson. Katy was absolutely comfortable with contradiction or multiple versions of events. She gathered many, many truths on the path to one story. She could hold them together and then work with the storytellers to take meaning from their versions of events. In some ways, this openness to more than one truth made it easier to spot deliberate or planted lies. Katy was utterly dogged in tracking down the soldiers present on the day and, perhaps ironically, it was these testimonies of veterans that were often closest to those of the families and the survivors. Something else also emerged – that actually, the two truths most likely to merge and harmonise, and have a common middle ground, would be the ones at the opposite ends of the spectrum. The worst of enemies would often agree that something was true. Often, the truths of the two sides would coalesce. The mud in the waters came from the state-sanctioned cover-up.

This taught me that all of life's big events weave a complicated set of multiple, conflicting narratives. People hold on to their own narratives but often many are squashed. It's always worth looking at who is getting to tell the story and where exactly the truth is coming from. It will probably always feel imperfect, but sometimes a compromise is necessary. Think of the divorced parents, boiling with righteous hurt, who know they have to find a way to co-exist so they can co-parent to raise their much-loved children. Or the employer who knows that redundancy will save their community-interest company but that some of their employees will never forgive them.

The necessary truth

Then there are those times when the narrative verdict is not right. When the brave thing is to stand up and push for One Truth. During my university years, I interned for Dr Phil Scraton at the Centre for Crime and Social Justice at Edgehill University. He was emerging as a leading campaigner alongside the family support groups fighting for justice after Hillsborough. This was 1998, and the Hillsborough families and survivors were mid-war, fighting against a series of lies that the state and branches of the media had perpetuated. For a long time and most of the time, louder, state-sanctioned narratives tend to win after disaster.

Within moments of the tragedy unfolding, police officers and specifically the match commander had allowed a lie to be perpetuated that fans had forced a gate into a tunnel and then entered already crowded pens. In fact, it was the commander himself who later admitted to ordering the gate to be opened. Even as the deaths were occurring, this lie was being briefed out and quickly spread around the world.

But the families tenaciously kept regrouping and trying again to tell their truth. Every last bit of energy was exhausted on another potential option within the torturous English legal system. Private prosecutions, more reviews, inquests and re-openings of inquests. Public inquiries. Judicial reviews. Meanwhile, amongst the families, there were divorces and further deaths; suicides and fragmentation of the support groups. One campaigner suggested to me that not being believed does something to the person, that it alters the brain chemistry and harms them perpetually, but what choice did they have but to keep going?

Phil Scraton's work embarrassed those in policing and sporting authorities by highlighting the number of football-stadium near misses and smaller-scale disasters that had happened in the years before. Phil had tracked down as much detail as he could about these. His university bosses repeatedly told him during this time that if he ever wanted to get ahead and stop pissing people off, he would need to drop his obsession with this one disaster and broaden his research career. Start playing the game, they would counsel, a plea many academics know well.

As well as teaching me about the energies needed for a difficult, precarious career, time with him was also an early lesson about the costs of this work. He was gaslighted constantly. He received a number of credible death threats against him and his children. It is a very lonely place on the right side of history. But he kept going.

I watched how he juggled multiple parties, all who had a story. Retired South Yorkshire police officers who had carried their version of events, that senior officers had then forced them to redact and alter, for over a decade, would find their way to Phil's office on the Ormskirk campus, dropping in bundles of notes and, in one case, evidence of redacted statements, when their words were changed by senior officers. Phil remembers that the former police officer 'went out to his car and he came back and he put a box file down and I opened it and there was his statements in three different forms with 53 sentences removed. I looked at this and I couldn't believe what I was seeing.'[26]

Professor Scraton went on to track down every statement he could. His book *The Truth* was his account of this and many other aspects of the disaster. He advised a number of film makers and went on to become the lead author of the Hillsborough Independent Panel Report, which fundamentally changed perceptions of the disaster and rewrote the truth for all to know.

The omnipresent bias of hindsight routinely pollutes how we come to talk about disasters. Following the release of the panel's report and the subsequent coroner's hearing that proved what the families and survivors had been saying all along, the story of their fight was reframed as if justice was some sort of inevitability. That the truth was bound to come to light. However, this washes away years of fight and pain. It ignores the cost of each stage of the struggle to get to the truth. It erases the fact that for much of that time those shouting that the authorities had got it wrong or were deliberately lying were simply not believed.

In such situations as this, where the version of the truth put out by the state or powerful organisations varies so widely from what was experienced by those who were there, who suffered, each new attempt at seeking justice is brutal. Every challenge to the accepted narrative takes family groups and survivors right back to their initial nightmare and starts a process of harm all over again. As the Liverpudlian journalist Brian Reade wrote later: 'Every time a culpable party tried to squirm out of taking responsibility, the families were dragged back to the beginning of their nightmare. They could never move on.'[27]

I will never forget the catharsis that came with the publication of the Hillsborough Independent Panel Report in September 2012. Not only were the families and campaigners proved right on so many key facts but also were allowed access to the methods that were used to deliberately marginalise and bury their stories. There can be some minor uncertainties around specifics of the day but what this report did was once and for all say loudly 'you were right'. As with many profound miscarriages of justice and abuses of power there *needed* to be a firm, righteous determination of what had actually gone before. Calling out the lies enabled some healing.

Truth and reconciliation

Something we also have to get used to challenging is the idea of forcing an agreement and an adherence to one truth only, in circumstances that are complex and difficult.

I have thought a lot about the enforced attempts by new governments or international courts to impose concepts of truth and reconciliation onto a grieving populace. Many of my colleagues work in the arena of forensics after human rights abuses and they bear the scars of this process. It is supposed to be that after one truth is agreed then reconciliation can begin. This has been a common feature of places that have known ethnic cleansing, genocide and mass inhumanity, such as Rwanda and Bosnia. In order to 'hold the truth', those governments have often made questioning or discussing the past events illegal too. We have seen more and more of this type of censorship in state policy making around the world but what I have learned is it never stops the questions being muttered or dispels the tensions sitting just below the surface like lava.

We are sometimes forced to bury certain truths on a personal level too. There have been several occasions in my working life that have brushed me up against extremely unpleasant people. For some time, I would have to listen to them being feted or held up as the new hero, even if they made me feel unsafe or compromised. My mum would counsel with one of her favourite phrases that 'it all comes out in the wash' – the truth would out, eventually. And generally, it has. But those interregnum periods before the narrative flips are exhausting.

I have seen survivors up close on the morning after a TV show has aired, a report has been published, a predator outed, a trial verdict overturned. The day they get to be believed once and for all. They are not as jubilant as the media want them to be. There may be some relief but there are often so many other emotions too. Exhaustion. Gut-wrenching frustration that it took that long. Vindication mixed with fear that the narrative might flip again.

If this speaks to you, if you are living through an interregnum period of truths – trying to co-exist with a really bad boss that the top brass thinks is great, or trying to warn a girlfriend off somebody you know is bad news – then hold hard. Protect yourself and know that you will already have done enough. Sometimes it is important to know when to exit and protect yourself.

If the situation is work based, or related to dealings with an organisation, there are practical things you can do that might help you in the future. For example, keeping records – emails, messages, notes on dates and time – in case you one day need to be able to explain your version of events. Beyond this, sometimes all you can do is wait and see.

Pogroms and riots

On the 29 July 2024, three little girls, similar ages to my own, were stabbed in a holiday dance workshop in the seaside town of Southport. Online posts triggered a wave of disorder across English towns and into Northern Ireland. Southport was a place that had struggled economically for some years and with areas of significant deprivation. When I met the responders there in the aftermath, I got to hear just how rough the pandemic had been on communities. There had also been concerns for years about racial tensions and there was growing evidence that far right groups were also stoking tension across the country.

Historically, as a pandemic wanes, the pogroms and the rioting begin. Working in the aftermath of emergency response, you learn a lot about temporality. Four years is about the right amount of time after chronic disaster to foment the conditions needed for an overboil, particularly when so many communities have been marinading in austerity for fourteen years. That timeline works at home too. We can endure chronic stress (such as a toxic relationship or work environment, or being an unpaid, unappreciated carer) for a few years before both our bodies and minds start to break down. There were other factors too. My work has always brought home to me how desperate some parts of many governments are to keep seething tensions under the surface. We come up with simple explanations when the realities are so much more complicated. We like to pretend that racism, sexism and classism don't riddle us. So when violence erupted on the 30 July 2024, I was far from surprised.

Tens of people were prosecuted for acts of violence in Southport in the coming months and for the rioting that spread to many other towns. Governments and some political commentators minimised what we were seeing as the actions of one very small and aberrant minority. Quite rightly, the disgust at both the levels of violence and overt racism were called out. But I continued to worry that certain truths were being varnished or neatly packaged. The youngest person convicted was eleven years old. Children who are so often rendered completely voiceless most of the time. But I also knew that rioting, however problematic, is a form of complicated communication and a marker in a country's history. It's the ultimate, terrifying explosion of multiple truths and requires a much more nuanced explanation. Professor Tim Newburn, an expert in criminology and social policy, warned that UK politicians wanted quick, simple and often weakly evidenced answers to the riots but actually almost nothing was done to address the multitude of problems the riots illuminated. He wrote, 'The danger is once again that the government will fail to investigate the events and will consequently fail to act. Now is the time for proper reflection. Not for lazy assumptions, or presuming that what we've seen on our screens means that we somehow understand all that has happened and know what, if anything, needs to be done.'[28]

I am certain that the way ahead for us all lies in truly understanding the burden that comes with living through a difficult time. The honesty required. There is a juggling of all the different truths at once that is migraine-inducing. If you think you are being pushed towards one truth, then there is a lot to be said for curiosity. You can agree that rioting and racism is wrong (one truth) while simultaneously believing that some of the anger, particularly expressed by children, has a need for exploration (another truth). The truths can and should be held together.

Not knowing

Our new ways of living, often circling around social media or mainstream media platforms, have forced stark stance-taking, boxing us into defending one position.

As we headed into the pandemic, and certainly in the incidents I have been involved in since, governments, police forces and scientists have tried to provide only one truth. Simplified and condensed down, rinsed free of the nibbling uncertainties. Pretending that science has the answers, or that authority could bestow total clarity on to a situation. For someone in a senior position to state simply 'we don't know' or 'we may never know' had become a rare, precious and unusual thing. It is seriously frowned upon by those above them.

When I first started in my career, I was not usually alone if I pointed out the uncomfortable truth or the curve ball. I was part of a wild-card choir. It didn't mean I 'believed' the thing I was raising; I was simply flagging it as another truth that would need to be held in this situation. But over time, that approach has come to be seen as more and more aberrant. We have been coached recently that there is one truth. One official account. But not allowing the holding safely of more than one truth may be forcing us into extreme positions. Simultaneously, more and more ways to create and amplify misinformation have been created and weaponised.

Some people tried to unpick my position on the

lockdown during the pandemic. If I posted something on the harms of a terrible virus left unchecked, they would immediately remind me that I had posted an article that talked about the harms of restricting children's abilities to socialise just a day earlier.

I have noticed more and more that people have 'one truth' on a subject. You can be this, but you can't be this. And that even reading around the other thing can look somehow disloyal or flaky. But that is not going to ready us for what comes next. It also leads to alienation of vast swathes of our fellow people. Take the changing climate. We don't need to beat each other over the head on the specific reasons for the changes – those truths will emerge long after we are all dead. But we do need to prep for the consequences. We also need to meet people where they are and tie ourselves in fewer knots by first trying to force agreement on a unified set of politics. It might seem simplistic to say but in an initial disaster response, I have no politics, no pre-conceptions and I actually don't need to share one truth with the people who need me. The Queen's bath towels is one of a hundred examples of times that disaster responders worked alongside multiple narratives, but still do find a way to work alongside. That works in our own lives too. Sometimes I think we overstate the need for complete coalescence.

The coming years will see conflict and turmoil entirely fought over who gets to present the 'truth'. The real knack here is to stay very, very curious and, if you can, a little bit enigmatic. Listen a lot. Behave like a diplomat who can see the thing from every angle. In our own lives, pick your battles carefully. You will need all your energy for surviving: fighting may take joules that you simply do not have. There is a peacefulness that comes with forgiveness and acceptance. It is not always the right path – as we have seen in this chapter, some truths must be fought for – but sometimes it is necessary for readying for the life ahead.

Our own truths

Navigating two (or more) truths is something that lies at the heart of so many family crises. It is there in bereavement and in relationship breakdown and particularly in the aftermath of divorce. In all situations where all parties feel the need to be right and to be heard.

A lot of psychologists urge the use of 'compassion' at this point and counsel trying to see things from others' perspectives, unless the issue is something like sexual abuse or domestic violence. There will be times when you need to decide that a narrative verdict will work for you and times when you know it has to be the Truth. One red flag to definitely push back on is if the truth comes with coercion. You also have to be able to really honestly assess the toll that holding your position is having on you and the relationships around you.

If you do decide that you can live with a narrative verdict then it is back to some New Testament principles of turning the other cheek. You have to find a way to co-exist with the two truths (someone can be somebody else's nice guy but was never the right chap for you). I find it helps to think more like a child when it comes to friendships too – not holding on to too many hurts, not demanding explanations and just powering through to the next fun time.

Something that Katy taught me here was the power of good television in illuminating the stories of 'the other side'. She often captured the other person's humanity or perspective too. We often paint very one-dimensional pictures of the villain or the bad guy, but I remember being so struck with Phil's compassion towards the police officers that sought him out. He understood that it might have been hard for them to speak out in the toxic culture at the time and that they were afraid. He made it clear that he respected their bravery when they found the way to his door. He also did something else – he actively listened to their stories of the day and that shed a new perspective into *their* fears and their traumas, which allowed him and others to see them in a different way. He taught me that it's not just about speaking or advocating – a lot of work in crisis is about listening.

Allowing contradiction to flourish is Jedi-level listening skills. Acknowledging that somebody can be both scared by moving away to college and excited at the thought of moving away to college and allowing room for both. In a world that demands a filtered consistency, it can be a rebellious act to hold more than one truth. Sometimes you want somebody to just hold your coat while you go into battle with your righteous view. There are times for that, but I think more and more as we go out along our path, we will need a different way to live and to co-exist. Maintaining firm boundaries when necessary and knowing when to truth seek. But also finding ways to hold multiple truths and live gently with difference.

> ## *Your recovery kit*
>
> **Are your two truths making you ill?**
> The burden of living with different truths and stories can take a toll on our physical health and lengthen the time it takes to recover from illness. We should think more about the stories we tell ourselves when we are ill and how they may be shaped by the reactions of those around us. We may be unduly affected by other people's perceptions and biases – for example, around conditions like long-term fatigue. How could you write a different story and centre yourself, not these prejudices, within it?
>
> **Accept aspects of the world for the way they are.**
> Complicated, messy, infuriating, deeply unfair. We often try to force situations and people to our way of thinking, forgetting the value of acceptance. There will always be fundamental differences between us and separation. Accepting something

does not mean that you are tolerating it; it means that you are seeing it clearly and your responses are informed by that.

Buy yourself time.
Sometimes, to get a different point across you need to buy yourself time. Practise this. It may mean adopting a 'musing face' – metaphorically drawing your hand down your long beard or smoking on a peace pipe. Learn to use more phrases like 'I don't disagree, but . . .' and 'let me think on that'.

Enquire.
Be really open to learning more, including in situations when that might be difficult. If someone is giving me 'feedback' or criticism, I actively visualise removing the sting from the words like you do an actual bee sting from your leg. I try to see past the heat of the reaction to the words and identify if there is a valuable point that I can learn from them. (Which is most of the time!) When communicating with someone expressing a different view, practise saying their truths out loud, as a position or question. This can be a powerful moment and may actually unite a group rather than alienating them.

Turn to the agony aunts.
I honestly don't know that I would be able to do my job without a lifetime schooled by problem pages and advice columns. Read as many as you can.

I recommend using something we call in disaster studies 'isomorphic learning', where we look at the broader learning not just the specifics of it – so a volcano in Hawaii might tell us something about managing a flood in Morpeth. Even if the problem page problem appears outwardly to be dealing with something you have not experienced, still take time with the answer as there is often a universal theme of trying to navigate multiple truths. It's a skill we all have to master, that's relevant in work issues, relationship breakdown and legal processes. They are also great at crafting ways to disagree sensitively or find the words to open a difficult conversation.

Look gently and kindly at yourself and your communications with other people.
Try to bring yourself to look at a situation from a number of different angles and seek advice on this. Helping a friend with a dispute with a colleague recently, I very carefully and with permission (she is a very good and tolerant friend) played the role of the other party. She realised that she might have fallen into a bit of a trap of tit-for-tat behaviour and there were probably some things she could try to do differently.

Be prepared for others to simply not want to carry on with a campaign.
This is advice I often give when addressing campaigners because I see so many families

damaged and couples split up over the best way to honour a quest for justice or change. This seems to be particularly true where bereavement is involved – families can feel torn over the amount of time they are giving to a fight and whether they have the energy or support to go on. It applies to many things in life, such as consumer or disability activism or working for a charity. My advice is always to try to compartmentalise it a little and make space for yourself, for lighter times and holidays, and for other family members. I also advise on carefully adjudicating events you are being invited to and watching out for whether you are being exploited. If you are asked to speak about your traumatic experiences or bereavement, I am very firm that your expenses and fees should be covered and events should be managed so as not to re-traumatise you. Build in your own dispensability and ensure that more than one of you can make the same points if you can't make it. Many bereaved parents confide in me that they exhaust themselves by turning up to everything because they feel like vital messages will get lost if they do not.

Lesson Eight
Survivance

I smile at eight-year-old Stanley's hands. They are bright green. Like a tiny version of the Hulk's hands. He waves them, palms front, at me. 'It's green for Grenfell day,' he says with a huge grin. 'There is always green paint everywhere on Grenfell day.'

Stanley is not wrong. There are palettes of green paint, tubs of green pens and a pre-printed green transfer that can be ironed onto a t-shirt. At the Henry Dickens community centre, there is a cacophony of noise as children select their activity. The adults' eyes are sombre and wary, but the children are delighted with themselves and with all the green. I laugh again at Stanley's hands and I marvel at his spirit. This is survivance.

Trying to keep going after the batterings of loss is one of the hardest things you will ever have to do. By 2007, 'recovery' was the word that we were supposed to use in UK emergency planning for the stage after the big impact. But I started to worry about it a lot and, more importantly, so did the many disaster-affected communities I was working with. It sounds so formal, so finished, affected communities would chastise. When I did my conference talks, I would use 'recovering' to convey the ongoing work that the communities were still needing to do. But that didn't really work either. I needed something else.

I first encountered the word 'survivance' when I presented research into how people come back from the grim losses of flooding at the US Federal Emergency Management Agency Higher Education conference in Washington in 2009.

On the last day of my trip, I took the opportunity to visit the Smithsonian Museum and noticed a large wall hanging that included this term in an exhibition about the ongoing struggle faced by Indigenous Americans. Underneath, it explained that survivance meant more than survival: 'Survivance means redefining ourselves. It means raising our political and social consciousness. It means holding on to ancient principles while eagerly embracing change. It means doing what is necessary to keep our cultures alive.'[29]

I saw straight away that I had found a word that did so much more than the official UK government lexicons. This was an active word, a doing word as my primary school English teacher would say. The poet Diane Glancy, of Cherokee descent, took the word further and focused in on the 'vivance' – the vitality of the word. There was the work of surviving but there was energy too. Survivance has *viva*, 'alive', right at the heart of it.

I was visiting the Smithsonian at a time in my own life when survival after loss was dominating both my working life and home. England had a massive rebuild underway from devastating flooding in the summer of 2007. It was also trying to pretend that it had healed from battling foot and mouth disease. Although this had been six years earlier, it had left terrible scars on agricultural communities. The battle against this disease had seen ongoing harm in some of the most beautiful parts of this island and over six million animals slaughtered in a seven-month period. The human suicides started about a year after the acute stage of culling flocks and herds. The data for those had just started to come in. The method was usually a shotgun.

The government was also trying to do that thing that Britain always does after disaster, like a Jack Russell attacking a pitbull, punching above its weight. It was trying to once again style out the idea that these disasters don't hurt us, not really. We'll be fine. Give us a week and everything will be open again. The UK's Labour government had rolled out a new set of training tools to ensure 'recovery from emergency' and I think I was already starting to lose a bit of faith in them. They were too formulaic. They strove for perfection, like an exacting sports coach's plan for his errant athlete a few months before the Olympics. The definition of perfection was that things would be at least as good as before the disaster and maybe even better.

I see people beat themselves up all the time that they don't seem to be able to get back to the way they were before. Let's face it – almost all of us are guilty of 'Jack Russell' behaviour. Going again. Failing to rest. Trying to convince those around us that they are not really seeing the bags under our eyes or the stress eczema on the backs of our hands. We are doing absolutely fine, thank you very much.

While I earned a living training people on these tools and talking about them, they never sat quite right. They just did not seem to fit with what I saw in the flooded communities that were trying to rebuild across the UK. A dot-to-dot that simply did not reflect the messiness. I particularly struggled with the idea (so fabulously New Labour) that somehow it could almost be spun that the disaster was a good idea for the place after all. That the terrible events had actually prompted regeneration and rehabilitation. Those words are literally right there in the Cabinet Office definition. They obliterated the work that was done by the survival communities themselves. I realised that I didn't want perfect.

Laughter in the dark

From the day a world explodes, there is a prescription for what life after loss, tragedy, disasters big and small, should look like. It is supposed to be heavy and miserable. But I have learned that this is often wrong. Some of the best belly laughs that have ever roared through my intestines have been at vigils, prompted by the best comedic lines I have ever heard delivered, deadpan, by the survivors and the newly bereaved.

Yet I have also noticed a curious trend to police the grief these people are feeling. To expect them, heads utterly fuzzy from shock and denial, still wondering if all this is some elaborate prank, to conform to a preconceived set of behaviours. Wearing black, looking sad, not going for a wild swim. Once I knew how to spot grief policing I saw it everywhere, and social media is terrible for it. Bereaved mums particularly are in the firing line of the grief police. Even when we think we are being kind and commenting on their bravery, there is an extra sting in the tail. 'I couldn't do what you do,' we say, with our heads tilted. Which implies that if we were grieving, we would feel it harder or deeper, our grief would take a more meaningful form which would render our legs useless. I have known women tear themselves apart over lines that imply that they are somehow so much stronger – does that mean that they are not feeling the loss as acutely?

It gets worse. 'Did you see those two mothers laughing together?' snipes a commentator on X, referring to two recently bereaved parents. Those smiles may even go on to be used as the starting point in elaborate threads and blog posts that the event itself, the shooting or the air crash, didn't even happen. People's own desperate attempts at coping are turned against them. Long before social media, I have known conspiracy theories proliferate in the aftermath of disaster. But the internet provides compost for them to spread and thrive in seconds. Everything from school shootings to a child's death in a war is pored over and picked apart as to whether it is true.

I learned long ago that it is never our right to censor how people process their own trauma or what comes next. Survivance after disaster is entangled with a dark, bitter humour – a humour that is as hard to capture as mist, here one minute and gone the next. I am asked a lot about humour from responders, and that's different. A necessary self-deprecation and then sometimes a darker gallows humour that I am much less fond of. But true survivance humour is like wasabi. It does so many things at once; as it comes out, it's electric but burns the oesophagus and the mouth. The target of the joke may be the absurdity of the situation, a moment of unintentional hilarity provided by the circumstances or maybe the responders. One of the things that people find most surprising about my work is the noise of that necessary, scalding laughter. Always followed by a furtiveness. Is it OK to laugh?

I think about the women of the disaster communities that I have spent so many afternoons with and the raucous, brutal nature of their joke-telling. The laughing does something. It is a physical action like coughing that releases the chalky pain we are holding on to in our glottis and lungs. It is a necessary and bodily catharsis. In New Zealand, following the 2011 earthquake, they even captured these acidic jokes – laughing at the absurdity of the response and recovery – into a joke book that they sold to raise money for affected communities.[30] Word plays about being shaken and not stirred.

Disasters often hit unequally and trounce a community already used to tough times. They batter the already hardest hit. But there is a fight back that begins at home and often with a joke.

'What else can we do but keep going?' shrugged the mothers of Toll Bar, who had lost everything in flooding, water up to their kitchen work surfaces. They had to put the tea on, get some paint back on those walls, build a new bookcase for the toys donated, print some photos off and place them carefully into plastic frames. 'I had a whole picture wall but it's gone now . . .' These families already knew that there is no signed contract that life owes us anything.

The council built them a communal laundry with top-of-the-range washing machines. Somebody added a noticeboard and a kettle and they went there even when all the washing was done. The acid laughter needs walls – the Henry Dickens Community Centre, north-west London, the laundrette in Doncaster, fishing huts in Sri Lanka, the Gresford chapel, the portacabins in Amatrice and the parishes of New Orleans. These places and spaces are not grand. The Women of the Storm group, which became a powerful lobby group after Hurricane Katrina, met in each other's kitchens to begin with. These places are essential in the rebuild and for living with the knowledge that disaster can come again so easily. Flood defences can only do so much. The women of Doncaster know that their homes may flood again. All they can do is keep going. Putting a wash on. There is a substantial body of research within the disaster literature on the role of women's movements in that early activism and momentum. Over decades, researchers have captured the 'bricolage', the hidden emotional labour that goes into the doing of the work in the weeks and months after disaster.

We all need to know that it is OK to laugh – in the cancer ward, in the hospice, at the funeral. My family is still chuckling at how Tom and my brother-in-law, Rick, very nearly dropped my dad's coffin (he was not a small man) when its solid structure and ample proportions took them both by simultaneous surprise. I am delighted to live in a world that is starting to embrace all sorts of new ways to be OK with difficult times. Applause at a memorial service. People with life-ending illnesses who hold FUN-erals to have a party that they can attend rather than a wake. Booking a comedy show straight after a serious hospital appointment.

Allies

Many years after my visit to the Smithsonian, in the spring of 2019, my husband Tom started to complain of headaches, loss of balance, vertigo and dizziness. He would look like a ballerina warming his feet up, waggling them, before going en pointe as he tried to work out where to place his feet on the floor in front of him. This would have been worrying for anybody, but as he was an airline pilot, we desperately needed it to be a short-term, fixable thing. They scanned him for tumours and assessed him and eventually diagnosed an atypical Ménière's disease, vestibular migraine and significant hearing loss. He would never fly again and his world changed forever. As the Covid-19 pandemic unfolded, we were already inside our own mini-disaster.

How all of us survive is highly individual. I tried to fix Tom using my own strategies. Lots (and lots) of talking, reading, boxsets of political comedy (*The Thick of It*), comfort eating, kitchen discos. Power ballads (I call them my #planthems). Things that had worked well for me in the 2000s, brought me my babies, and still work now.

But none of them were working for Tom. I was getting this wrong.

It was an important and simple realisation that you have to be guided to survivance, slowly, to find what works for you. Maybe that is why the term 'survivance' defies easy definition. It cannot be thrust upon you by outsiders and there is no one definitive prescription.

About fifteen months after Tom's diagnosis, I realised with a jolt that I had not really heard him laugh for all of that time. I couldn't remember what his real laugh actually sounded like. Only the one that was forced through his teeth when he knew he was supposed to laugh. The first time I heard that laugh again properly was when he was surrounded by a few of his own male friends. A couple of them were battling their own new health diagnoses and in the process of figuring out what that might mean for their own careers and lives. They signed up for half marathons. They went camping. A peer support group, a place and a survivance ritual was formed that is now a regular event.

My friends Anne and Jelena, a survivor of Hillsborough and a bereaved sister from 9/11, have written extensively about peer support groups in the aftermath of disaster. Like everything, for them to be given weight by the politicians and scientists, these groups had to be measured and evaluated and evidenced. Which has proved repeatedly what seems so obvious. People who have been through what you have been through can be a vital part of survivance. Making a space, either online or physical, for those people to come together can fundamentally help. In quiet rooms hired from libraries and museums, with a supply of good quality biscuits and topped-up tea urns. These peer support groups nurture the chance to talk and to laugh. To make the jokes that only those who are walking the same path can make.

A key part of survivance is to find the sort of peer support that works for you. There are many examples of the value of this sort of support in all areas of our lives. Health peer support, maternity peer support, debt, depression, addiction.

In 1991, a group of men and women, both bereaved by UK disasters and survivors of them, formed Disaster Action. This was a group designed to provide mutual support by people who had been through cataclysmic events, and also to inform responders how to improve the care of those affected by them. In the late 1990s, they allowed me to attend several of their events. It may come as a surprise that I would describe them as often strangely uplifting. The laughter flowed easily. It was in these spaces that people began to make sense of the events that they or their family member had experienced. Often, other relatives had clues to what had happened that no law enforcement agent had been able to answer. These were spaces where people could share details of resources and support groups and also cross-check the offers that they had received from authorities. They talked about how to deal with media requests and anniversaries.

The survivance shown by Disaster Action wasn't just about laughter and camaraderie in difficult times. It was about tackling the tough questions too. It had a particular knack for managing tensions within its own cohort, which has been the reason for many other activist groups to flounder. Everybody was acknowledged in the space and there was a watchful eye on any weaponisation of disaster hierarchies. Who had been closer or lost more. They juggled so smoothly and beautifully the inherent tensions that emerge between survivors and bereaved. Often survivors – of disaster, of cancer, of a near miss – can be enthusiastic and effusive. Can talk about how they feel chosen or saved, and have a new *joie de vivre*. This can be incredibly painful, jarring, for a bereaved family to hear. The organisers tackled this carefully and directly when they arranged events or press releases. Survivance requires looking issues in the face together and working towards a solution.

Who turns up for you can be surprising, and it may not be the allegiances you first expect. Friendships often reshape in extremis. A lot of the post-crisis research places great emphasis on the role of allyship and also advocacy and mentoring. Look for your allies in new places and think about what it is you might want from them. One of my greatest joys in the last few years has been making new acquaintances via online networks. Mum has found it unexpectedly helpful to follow the travails of women bereaved of their partner around the same time as her. She piggybacks my social media to check that they are alright. She says it feels like they get it and when they try something different, a new coping strategy, she will give that a go too.

Roaring back

I am called into another meeting about the children of Grenfell. These children watched their friends die in the tower, texted them from their bedrooms and stayed as the sun rose on the inferno praying that they had got out. Some, in intense physical shock, pulled on their blazers and their ties and went to school at 9am that day. The children who were ten at the time are now seventeen. They have always had strong, eloquent voices and now they wield them like Arthur's sword. There is a growing concern from certain responders, certain agencies, that the children have started to do something naughty. They have agreed with the adults, the gatekeepers, to say certain things at the meetings and events. A script is crafted. Then, when the children get in front of the camera, onto the stage, under the lights of the event where they can no longer be controlled, they are saying something else that is not written down. Saying other words entirely, turning their righteous anger on those who killed their friends. I am immediately put in mind of one of the best survivance songs I know – Tim Minchin's 'Naughty' from the musical *Matilda*, with its lyrics that celebrate the necessity of sometimes not doing what you are told if something is not fair.

What can be done about it, the officials asked me? A broad grin spreads across my face. Absolutely nothing can or should be done about it. This is absolutely marvellous. This is where my own brand of survivance will always be at odds with official ideas of what recovering looks like. I love what these young people are doing. The wiliness. The rebellion. It is infused with Scouse-level cheekiness that makes me deliriously proud. I say all this in the meeting and the officials look horrified, muttering about safeguarding. I know I won't be invited back but I leave the meeting with a smile and a spring in my step. The kids are OK.

Threatened communities have every right to stick their middle figures up at those sent to help them. To roar back at them. They get to tell their own stories. They get to laugh on their own terms. How communities are supposed to come back is policed and sanitised and I have come to adore the rebellion from laughing eyes underneath heavy fringes.

And that there is the final, crucial, part of the lesson of survivance for all of us. Its middle finger. I am well known for my love of the survivors' aberrance, their mischief. I am also becoming more and more well known for my own defiance within my industry and maybe at home too. It constantly places me at odds with the official plans because I simply will not agree to try and manage the defiance away. When they refuse to attend the government's official anniversary event and instead stage something of their own in the park around the corner. When they sing a protest song in their own language when the responders turn their backs. I think about a group of mothers holding the keys to the Henry Dickens centre hostage while smoke still billowed from a mass grave. They took direct action, taking power back along with their space. 'We felt at once we could be in control of our own recovery and support those around us. Once neglected, our community centre was now lovingly cared for, windows and floors cleaned and scrubbed, we watched over the building like a baby. In the days after the fire, after we had established art therapy groups and a space for the children to come after school.'[31] The fight was on.

I take inspiration every day from these moments of defiance. If I know I have a difficult meeting that morning I will listen, on loud, to Stormzy's rap about Grenfell performed at the Brit Awards in 2018, highly critical of the government's response to the disaster. This was even naughtier than it first may have appeared. He, like the children of Grenfell, rehearsed to different lyrics so his performance would not be pulled if word got out that he was going to do it.

I will always struggle with ideas like post-traumatic growth or recovering. They feel too close to the idea that the bad thing was good for us. But I do totally get the idea that we are made by these events and the persons and the communities may have new strengths unlocked because of them. Many men and women take decades and decades to become the person they were always meant to be and sometimes these life events can accelerate that. Sudden ill health or a major life change can eventually unlock some wonderful devilment that was there all along. Modern life involves a lot of behaviour policing and suppression. But the clarity of survivance strips much of that away. People are then freed to be their truest selves, more of what they already were.

> ## *Your recovery kit*
>
> **Children's survivance needs specific thinking.** Children are not little adults. They are also not future adults. They have their own identities, needs and voices. We keep our children young and try to protect them, but often they are more capable than we know. I am grateful to my work with Save the Children and the CUIDAR project at Lancaster University, which was child-led and focused on emphasising that children from the youngest of ages need a much greater voice in emergency planning and response.
>
> How children and adolescents have experienced the pandemic is particularly important to understand because of something called epigenetics. This is the science of how adolescent genes are activated and affected by experiences: 'Experiences very early in life, when the brain is developing most

rapidly, cause epigenetic adaptations that influence whether, when, and how genes release their instructions for building future capacity for health, skills, and resilience.'[32] In order to 'power through' the last few years, we have been worryingly dismissive of how much we have changed the actual minds and bodies of our children and adolescents. We now have to do the hard yards to repair that.

Talk openly with children about what has happened and don't censor them. Some of the toughest questions I have ever answered on fire safety and emergency response have been from the children of the Henry Dickens centre. Involve children in discussions of emergency plans. Both of my kids have grab bags and hurricane lamps.

Think about whether you are shutting children out during a family crisis or limiting opportunities for them to express themselves or their needs.

Don't be offended by a family member's 'setbacks'.
Often an illness relapse or a recurrence of depression can make you feel like you are somehow failing the person. Return to the recovery graph and remember that the uptick can be fragile and place people back inside the slump.

Ground yourself.
Literally imagine your feet planting hard into the ground, weighed down, and grip onto a surface with both hands. This steadies and readies us.

Use music.
I post about our emergency planning #planthems a lot. This is music that we use to ready ourselves for a tricky meeting or a difficult day.

Go outside.
Some form of nature-bathing has featured in the healing from all of the disaster aftermaths I have ever seen. Scrunching bare feet into grass or sitting under a forest canopy. I remember learning from the emergency planners at a number of college campuses in the USA that had suffered shootings. They said that the students wanted to be outside all the time and sit under trees. They even moved the lessons out there. It has been under-prioritised in our pandemic response so far but it is probably one of the most important things to consider in school and early years settings, and for adults too. Studies evaluating the Japanese art of 'forest bathing' (*shinrin-yoku*) have shown its positive physiological effects, such as blood pressure reduction, improvement of autonomic and immune functions, as well as psychological effects of alleviating depression and improving mental health.[33]

Have fun.
Look again at how you are building fun, lighter times into your diary. Emergency planners often struggle with big blocks of leave, but we really try to protect people's long weekends away or afternoons off. Don't ever feel guilty about building more fun into your diary.

Lesson Nine
Painting Your Kintsugi

Jan from the Track and Trace helpline sat on the phone for hours talking to Ari. His wife was in the hospital with Covid and the news was getting worse by the hour. Ari had tested positive too, but he couldn't understand why he only had a sore throat and conjunctivitis and she might lose her life. It was a question puzzling the whole nation at the time.

Jan was only supposed to work from a pre-agreed script but she didn't feel able to leave Ari. Her main role was to check in with individuals who had recently tested positive for Covid-19 and their contacts, but there was a second part of the script where helpline staff could see if someone needed any help and had access to medical advice.

Ari was becoming more and more distressed and eventually Jan put him on speakerphone so that her supervisor could alert the police to check on him. Ari sobbed and pleaded, becoming agitated. He explained that his wife was all he had. One son died in infancy and another was killed in a car crash in his native

Bulgaria. He was crying so hard that it sounded like choking.

There was a special pathway to activate the police to conduct a welfare visit – the first stage would be to talk through the door and they would wear full PPE to do it. They checked on Ari and spoke to the hospital, and later Jan was able to check back in on him too. He wanted to talk to her again when his wife was discharged and even thanked her for being there. It was a story with a happy ending.

But when I met with Jan, several weeks later, she was struggling to sleep. She told me about Ari and his wife in big breaths. She didn't know what Ari looked like but in her mind she had cast him as big and bearded. She worried that she didn't do enough. She struggled with the idea that Ari was one of the good news stories – so why were his sobs in her dreams now? She had other stories by then – such as ringing a positive-testing new dad whose partner and baby were both dangerously ill in hospital, severely damaged by the infection and then sepsis. She knew that some of the men and women she had spoken to didn't make it.

The Track and Trace system, used to support testing and isolating people with coronavirus, has become infamous for its bureaucracy and for not providing value for money. It became the butt of a hundred jokes on satirical political comedy shows. But I got to see a very different side of it in 2021 when I was asked to meet with a group of the tracers as part of a 'wellbeing' session. It was organised in local areas and the staff, mainly women, had signed up from within health organisations and the local authority. They had never thought of themselves as frontline disaster responders. But I told them that was exactly what they were and their eyes grew larger. I was meeting them online, making it hard to read the room, and impossible to reach across and touch an arm, but I could tell that calling them that had shocked them. I talked about the disaster recovery graph and what it was normal to feel as a responder. But they fought me because this wasn't a disaster and they hadn't done very much really. They were hurt by becoming the target of political jokes and by all of the national rhetoric that they had not been there at all. When they were described as a waste of money, the words landed like arrows. But most of all they were haunted by the voices. Particularly when they found out later that they were the last person to speak to someone before they died.

My worry for them was that research showed that actually sometimes some of the worst trauma comes when all we can do is listen. It was no surprise to me that the phone calls had burrowed into their heads. That the voices had become startling interruptions in their new working days. First, I told them they needed to admit that this was something that had an impact. I was capable of working through that bit with them. But when it came to the way that the phone calls were haunting their dreams, I would need to call in the cavalry in the form of trained therapists.

We all have wounds – some of them our own and some of them imprints we have received from holding others up. This is about painting our wounds gold and fixing them back together. This lesson is named after the Japanese art of kintsugi, the mending and enhancing of broken pottery with golden paint. The scars become as important as the original material, the broken pot not thrown away but celebrated for its brightly coloured healing. Kintsugi leaves cracks visible, golden and shining. They are something to be proud of, something to even be displayed.

This captures something perfectly for me because I wear my scars with pride – literally and metaphorically. My own brushes with ill health and also with baby making mean that I have scars on the top of my head, my breasts, many across my abdomen inside and out, my groin, both knees, one foot. I wear them like jewels. Painted a metaphorical gold. The greatest part of painting your kintsugi is recognising that you are a much better survivor than you have ever given yourself credit for. But the first step is that the pottery has to be glued back together before those joins can be painted.

Phantoms

Their faces would appear at the worst possible moment. When I was looking at my husband Tom. Side on. In our bed. As he reached for me. His face would morph into theirs and my first thought would be confusion. Then horror. And I knew that I needed to work on asking them gently and respectfully to leave us be.

Flashbacks are probably one of the best-known ways that we bring the things we are trying to process home.

They are powerful, not a memory but somehow still right there, and can be destabilising and upsetting. They provoke the same and sometimes even more of the stress hormones that occurred with the original event. I have come to recognise the look on friends' faces when they have just dragged themselves out of one.

One thing that can help is addressing the flashback directly – 'Ah, here you are again, reminding me of something that is in my mind. But you are a memory and you are not real.'

So I would blink hard and address the memory head on, and Tom's face would morph back to his actual face, no longer a reminder of the dead man I had spent the day caring for. Then I looked for his eyes.

I fell in love with Tom's eyes before anything else. The deepest, honest wells that contain no guile or malice. Previously, I had known cheeky Scouse footballer eyes or a more toxic, macho gaze that understood only privilege and taking. But these eyes were something else. When I met Tom, he was a shy aeronautical engineering student, keen one day to be an airline pilot. I was a somewhat evangelical and 'passionate' law student. Some might say intense. We were in a houseshare, meeting in the first few days of our second year of university. I returned one night before term had even started from a disappointing night in a friend's new flat to Tom, still up, watching *Dr No* with the other housemates. And there were those eyes. Sean Connery faded into the background and I was completely smitten.

Our relationship, then and now, is surprisingly wordless. I talk *a lot* in my work so I think it comes as a surprise to people that we are so quiet together. But through him, I learned the meaning of the companionable silence. We connect now in the same way as we did in 1998, through touch and through finding each other. Tom became the only way that my brain, my head of bees that are my oldest companions, would go quiet. In that first winter together, as soon as the rest of the house was asleep, I would creep across the hall. In his arms and in his bed, I discovered something that has remained the key to shutting everything else out.

This medicine, this solace, is usually iron-clad against intrusion, but very occasionally, the day's work can sneak in. Traumatic flashbacks are strange beasts because there is literally no warning, no slo-mo. Just bang! and they are there. And all of a sudden, at the start of my career, when I lay down next to Tom his face would shift, CGI style, into those of the bodies I had been with that day. Well, that needed to stop.

Being adjacent to disaster, to trauma, for the whole of an adult life is something that needs careful and regular support and calibration. A key lesson this life has taught me is that there are people walking around every day unsupported, trying to process the things that they have experienced. Abuse and violence, crime, hospital and birth trauma. I am incredibly blessed that my career coincided with such an explosive growth of interest in how the brain and body processes difficult times. I give thanks daily that we can talk so much more freely than any other generation before about trauma. But despite this, when bad things happen to us, they rend our souls and our cells, and then often we try to pretend that actually nothing bad has happened at all. We may understand the damage better than ever, but the damage is still there.

The global, universal nature of the pandemic means that not only are we all survivors now, we are almost all supporters too – we know what it is like to calm our family's fears, to try to support our parents or neighbours, to lend a listening ear to those in loneliness or pain. The terrible toll of disease and austerity has also left many of us as carers.

I realise from the questions that I am asked when I give talks now that people are often deeply troubled. There are lots of questions about emergency responders' strategies, and specifically my own strategies for dealing with emotional trauma. I feel searching eyes trying to work out what is going on in my head. People sometimes comment that I seem more light-hearted than they expected, cheerier. There is nothing quite like that sort of scrutiny to make you reflect on your approach to your work. They want to know how I mended and I want to tell them about living alongside your scarring. And then painting it all gold.

The sense of a shared experience after the pandemic is profoundly different to anything I have experienced before. In July 2024, I found myself sharing a shady bit of a beach with an American family, who were on holiday too. After the briefest of small talk, we were swapping pandemic experiences as if we are kin. One common language. We talked about lockdowns and Boris Johnson and empty supermarket shelves. Then the grandma started to cry and the grandad worried at some skin in his hands, and they told me that they began to foster their grandchildren during the pandemic. They whispered to me all the ways that these little boys changed. By the time that our drinks arrived, I was showing them links on my phone for ways to help children after disaster.

It's taken a long time for the world to face up to the key fact that after disaster must come the reckoning. We are much more comfortable pretending that we can take things in our stride.

One of my early mentors, Eric, was a dentist and a key innovator of the practice of forensic odontology.[34] Practising dentists, who by day fill cavities and check teenage overbites, came to be deployed to mortuaries in the event of mass fatality incidents, and quickly established themselves as one of the greatest assets in early disaster identification work. Teeth and the inside of mouths survive when pretty much every other body part does not. Forensic dentistry was (and still is) a fast and popular mode of identification. Working with the mouth and the jaw of the deceased is incredibly intimate work, and also, I learned, incredibly physical. There have been many changes in practice but in order to get to the teeth once rigor mortis has set in, especially if there has been intense temperature applied to the face and bone, there often needs to be serious strength applied. Think about the noise that your jaw makes when it cracks and then times that by a thousand. Forensic dentists are very good and effective at what they do, and by the time I was working in this field too, they were used constantly and all around the world. They are often a very human connector between the incidents I work on. The same dentists that identified the dead of the New Zealand earthquake in 2011, the majority of whom were killed in building fires, are the exact same men and women who identified the dead of Grenfell Tower. But there is a toll to this work.

When Eric retired, he gifted me a back catalogue of his articles, his journals and the newsletters of the British Association of Forensic Odontology. In those pages, you can see, via the air disasters of the 1970s, 80s and 90s, the tentative, embryonic development of 'trauma support for responders' alongside articles on ageing the deceased by their teeth. There is sometimes a sense of revelation in the articles that working in this field might actually mean someone would require support. That you might need some extra help to sleep at night. That you might take what you had seen in the day home with you.

I am grateful that over the last thirty years, the thinking about the help we might need has continued to proliferate, legitimise and develop. We all need these lessons now. They are necessary for everyone as they make their way through the ups and downs of life. I have also realised how little this is taught and how much it can change a life to know these simple things.

It doesn't need to be because you work in forensics or mountain rescue. Lots and lots of people work in fields that may expose them to regular trauma – from care workers to hair stylists (now trained to spot signs of domestic violence and child abuse). Even more of us will encounter trauma-worms in our own lives – imagery or worries that burrow a bit deeper into our brain. Caring for a seriously ill relative or witnessing a partner having a difficult birth. Sometimes I wonder with some awe at just how many of us are walking around, trying to survive, wearing our trauma like saddle bags.

I also take issue with the idea that all seeing and experiencing has to be traumatic. We can see and experience difficult things, but we can sometimes tackle them in such a way that stops them becoming harmful. A few years ago, our little 'Jackadoodle' puppy Chaz managed to squeeze under our gate and was caved in under the wheels of a 4x4. Tom retrieved her body from further up the road, small enough to fit in a pillowcase, and our little girl Elizabeth begged to be allowed to see her. Half our dog's head was perfect, peaceful; the other half was missing, smashed by the car's hard, metal grilles. We made her a cardboard box bed coffin, best half-face upwards, and our three-year-old Elizabeth sat gently stroking her for what felt like hours. We answered every question Elizabeth had as best we could and she chose the flowers and tree for her grave. We filled Chaz's box with some favourite things for her journey and Tom set about digging her a hole.

One thought that guided me through that long night into day, was that many bereaved people had told me that the imagery their imagination cooked up was worse than any real imagery before them. This principle has always guided me. I say hi to the fears so that my imagination does not run off with them. Seeing Chaz was hard and it would be perfectly normal for her to appear in our dreams or even as brief intrusive flashbacks for the first few weeks. But my work has taught me that if those images had stayed, then we would need to ask for help.

What has worked for me

Over the years, I have honed a few things that help when I start to feel really burned out or disheartened. Growing flowers and plants that I can water. Pots of brightly coloured, random annuals that must be watered, rain or shine, at the end of a long day. These pots would go on to become ridiculously precious to me – woe betide anyone who tries to throw them out when they need kintsugi themselves, ravaged by frost. They move with us to every new house. The natural world knows the way. Seasons and the consistency of a growing calendar help. Knowing that whatever else is going on for us at the time, there is a cycle, and the first snowdrops will start to nudge out with no care for our deadlines or stresses, is important in healing. So start with plants and, if you are able, pets may be beneficial too.

Breathwork is important. When we are responding to a stressful and urgent situation, we often breathe short, shallow breaths, making us feel more panicked, like we are not getting enough air. It's possible to retrain our breathing, learning to breathe from the diaphragm

– intentionally and deliberately inhaling and exhaling, noticing how the stomach rises and falls as the diaphragm contracts and relaxes as air fills and is released from the lungs. Practising this in calm situations means we can more readily access this technique when we find ourselves in a time of stress.

I have very separate wardrobes: work clothes and home clothes. Work clothes are an armour that can be taken off and put away when it is time for fun. I also use music to help and I love to shake it off (I did this years before Taylor Swift) and throw myself around the kitchen to assorted dance tracks. I also listen to specific music before attending a disaster scene. I watch out for too much alcohol or a reliance on anything else 'unhelpful' to take the edge off.

I have learned to be on the look-out for one of the most potent flashback inducers, olfactory trauma, where smell becomes associated with a memory and bang, you are right back there. You can't always have control of that but there are times when you can pre-plan for it. I always tell pregnant friends to never take their favourite perfume or bodywash to the birth. Keep that as special and not necessarily related to this ideally wonderful but not always easy life event.

I used to find holidays anxiety inducing – anything where I was supposed to force relaxation for an extended period of time made me feel like I was rattling the disaster fates. But I have learned to enjoy the moment and not pack too much in. If an afternoon suddenly becomes free, I can usually resist the temptation to fill it with chores or other work. These moments are few and should be valued for the chance they give us to pause.

Recently, I have had the chance to talk to several of the psychologists who mentored me when I was in my twenties. Now they feel freer to express their protectiveness of me and particularly the fear they had that my enthusiasm would burn out and the joy I had in my work, the interest, would be overtaken by darkness and bitterness. I am so grateful for the time that they took with me then to help me make sure this didn't happen. These days, I work constantly to pay this help forward to those coming up behind me. This is an important lesson I think – look after yourself as the priority and extend that care to others as much as you are able.

Good therapy

But as helpful as I find the breathwork, the bright plants outside the window, the kitchen disco, all of this has not always been enough to banish these intruders from my bedroom. To deal with these flashbacks, I needed to talk. Some of my own kintsugi cracks were painted by trauma specialists who helped me to make sense of myself within this world. I would recommend that to anyone. I have always paid for it and always booked it in in the same way as I book in for my fancy cut and blow dry. It's a treatment and a service to myself.

I have been truly blessed to have found the best listeners in the world. I have benefitted from a range of different therapies over the years, usually cognitive behavioural therapy, but what has often been crucial for me personally is that the person working with me has seen some of the same things. One of the biggest mistakes I believe that I have seen the National Health Service make is to send brand new, young graduates to support grizzled, cantankerous responders in some of our recent disasters. The responder has confided in me afterwards that the person reminded them of their daughter and they simply could not hand over to her what was in their head at that moment. What it feels like to cradle somebody's head in your lap as their last life blood drains onto the tarmac. When they began to tell the psychologist about their day, they said, they saw the shock cross her face and linger in her eyes. So they censored themselves and made themselves iller.

Make sure that you find someone who works with you. The best talking therapy for my trauma came about when the person got to know me and even watched me at work. A true luxury that is rare in most therapeutic relationships, though, I realise. They had already spotted that what hurt me most was being made to keep quiet on some future harm being done by bureaucracy or poor processes to the grieving family, not the actual work itself. I would rather watch a colleague force a tiny body into their favourite pyjamas ten times over than watch them shred a piece of paper that explained how they died.

My listeners defragged my hard drive and made sense of the stories. They taught me to slow down. They helped me see things from colleagues' perspectives and gently guided me to explore how to protect myself from overthinking. They did something that was both anathema and vital. They reminded me, and all of us, that what I do is just a job. There is a peace and a humbling in remembering that.

People working in fields like mine are ripe for getting hurt badly. They are often empaths and over-thinkers. They often manage a generalised anxiety by releasing it through this work. There are high levels of vocational awe. This is where people are very invested in the idea that they are making a difference and feel validated, a little intoxicated and a bit special because of that. But this work is fickle and it actually doesn't love you back, despite its reputation as 'humanitarian'. The wrong people get the tea and medals.

I talk to my fellow responders about writing this lesson, and it triggers an unsurprising stream of memories and grimaces and methods that have worked for people. Alison remembers how difficult it was to come home after working in the mass graves of Bosnia. How petrified she would be that she might not have washed all the smell off her and her two wee girls might pull away. They would want to surprise her at the airport or coach station and she would beg her husband not to let them until she had one more Radox-infused bath. Mark walks for hours and hours, the tougher terrain the better, shouting into the wind. For Helen, it's rescuing cats. Nathan bakes.

Meredith goes swimming. A lot of us use water. I bob up and down in the swimming pool like a rowing boat that has broken free of its moorings. I should try to swim properly, get some blood flowing to the heart and the head, but I like the weightlessness of simply floating around. My bees like the water too and they still. I tip onto my back and forget that there are others in the pool, navigating around me like a wreck. I learned long ago not to use the roped-off lanes for serious swimmers for my trauma purge. The pool is where I come when I am most distressed and most overwhelmed. The bobbing is stage one of the Big Cry. After the Big Cry I book in with my therapist.

Many of my friends have had difficulties processing aspects of their lives or traumatic situations, and often pin their earlier, failed relationships on not being able to share this with a partner. At one talk I gave recently, a woman prison officer sidled up to me with a tired grin to say 'your book saved my marriage'. She recounted that during the pandemic, as prison conditions became even grimmer from a baseline of grim, she could feel herself changing. Her work had always been challenging but Covid stripped away all her coping mechanisms. There was no survivance laughter. They were not allowed to socialise with colleagues or stay for a chat. They could not see each other's expressions behind masks. The prisoners in their care acted from a place of fear and frustration, as the disease stalked the cells. She was exposed to constant self-harm and successful suicide attempts. She ploughed on at work but she did what a lot of us do and her pain came out at home. Onto those around her. She became what we technically describe in our line of work 'an arsehole' to live with. She was losing him, the man who kept her sane, who took away her own bees. I described that the hardest part of working in disaster is coming home, and she said that allowed her to unlock a conversation with him about how much she was struggling to make that transition. She tentatively opened a conversation with him as soon as she had finished the book.

And, as I mentioned earlier, I always advise appointing a 'burnout monitor' from your trusted kin. Somebody who can have that tough talk with you when you appear to be descending into arsehole territory. You might think you are coping magnificently, you may even be winning awards at work. You may be the person that everyone confides in. You may still be a party animal. But your behaviour may have massively changed at home, possibly without you realising.

Honing your inner voice

Don't look at me like I'm mad – it is absolutely essential that you are able to talk to yourself. It is one of the most important skills for improving your mental health and your ability to process what you have been through. There is a substantial evidence base for the idea that how you talk to yourself, inside your head, makes a profound difference to your emotional and physical wellbeing. As I told Jan and the men and women from Track and Trace sat with her, you have to be able to thank yourself. You also have to be able to forgive yourself. How many times do you let your inner voice tell you that you are doing great? When it comes to traumatic memory, this inner dialogue has a profound effect on whether you feel stable or overwhelmed.

I don't want anything I have said here to be taken as diminishing the need for support and understanding when trauma becomes a much more insidious post-traumatic stress disorder, which can affect about 10 per cent of survivors. One way to know you might need additional support is if your symptoms are still affecting life five or six months after the event.

For your kintsugi to shine, you must first admit that the joins that need painting are there. I had my work cut out with Jan and her team, but I knew they were worth the title of 'disaster responder' and I pleaded with them to not dismiss their own experiences. Minimising what you did, what you went through, is a common trait but a harmful one.

You need to learn how to do boundaried care – how to be an activist and a helper but without harming our own selves. Learning not to overpromise. I know now that it is essential (not selfish or luxurious) that you carve out time for yourself. In helping people with their mental health, the idea of 'putting your own oxygen mask on first' has become a popular analogy – repeating the safety briefing on a plane. It makes sense, I watch people nod sagely along to it in NHS 'wellbeing' training. Except caregivers don't do it. They struggle to assist their children or relative first, even other people, and then pass out from hypoxia. Be ruthless that you are an important person.

We all need ongoing maintenance for our kintsugi. Check in regularly for more gold paint and glitter. Painting that gold is about artistry and enhancement. There are so, so many different ways in which we can get chipped or cracked. There is also so much bewildering advice. And accessing support requires knowing how to get it and resources. But it really can be the difference between half-life and full-life, and that's worth trying to find.

Your recovery kit

Find therapy that works for you.
It can be hard to find the right type of therapy but start with www.bacp.co.uk. If you fall into a specific community of circumstance, such as being a victim of crime, a patient of a disease or a veteran, then support groups will signpost you. It may be that first person you find doesn't work for you. Know that it is OK to look around for another option, though do be aware of 'therapist shopping'. Go with the mindset that this should be a little bit challenging and gently confronting and should come with a little bit of homework.

It is important to open yourself up to the idea of healing.
Start small by exploring useful concepts. Buy, or ask for as a gift, magazines like *Psychologies* and

Simple Things. They have lots of advice on opening yourself up to ideas of analysing your behaviours and thinking about healing.

Evaluate your use of alcohol, drugs, nicotine and even prescribed meds.
I don't drink but I do overeat and can over-rely on painkillers for my poor health. Other addictions can creep in too (my worst is my phone) and that requires a regular audit. Be honest about your use of things that may be an unhelpful crutch.

Know what is 'normal'.
For a few days or weeks after a difficult time, it is perfectly normal to have bad dreams. Sometimes with bereavement, those dreams may start months later. I often think dreams are one of the most effective ways to work through certain things. What is not normal is to find that you are avoiding sleep or becoming incredibly distressed by the dreams. Good sleep is so important, so seek help early on if this is very disrupted. The same is true of anxiety – it is perfectly normal to feel worried or notice the world differently. But if you have stopped going out altogether or have become very obsessive it will likely be helpful to address this head on.

This is not a short-haul thing.
Often, I review plans that assume 'all the trauma' will appear and be dealt with in the first two years

after an incident. The disaster research actually shows that it can take decades to appear. It is OK to have to revisit things from much earlier in your life.

Lesson Ten
By Hammer and Hand

The fire is believed to have become unmanageable on that London night at about 1am. It began in a baker's shop on Pudding Lane on 2 September 1666 and quickly spread to nearby buildings. It burned for five days and devastated much of the city within the walls. We know from the contemporaneous diaries and papers of the time that it took into its flames at least 13,000 homes, 44 livery company halls, numerous warehouses, 87 churches, the Royal Exchange and St Paul's Cathedral.[35] At least six people died, although historians dispute this as many may have perished who were simply not counted or known about. Over 85 per cent of London's population became homeless immediately. The rebuild would be immense.

I think sometimes when we look back on historical disasters, we minimise the effects they had, perhaps comforting each other that it was 'different then'. That the loss of homes and personal effects meant something different to people of yore, who lived with a very difficult level of risk and precarity. But I have often thought about those Londoners as being no different from the citizens of many other evacuated places right here and now. I imagine *hiraeth* was as potent a feeling in 1666 as it is now.[36]

The order of priority that King Charles II gave certain things in the aftermath of the fire also seems very familiar. Documents suggest he was particularly concerned about the risk of rioting from the dispossessed refugees and encouraged their resettlement elsewhere. Fighting broke out on the streets as recently arrived foreign migrants, already subject to violence on the streets, were beaten up. Rumours had flown around that the fire had been started by them, and they were rounded up by soldiers in the following days. Post-disaster housing was as much of a problem then as it is now and people sheltered in fields on the outskirts. Some ended up staying there for years. A national fund was set up to coordinate charitable giving. And of course there was the inquiry.

And then it was time for the rebuild. It is fascinating to me that even in the way we now contemporaneously explain the fire, in websites and on museum information boards, we extol that the fire was an opportunity for regeneration. London's Science Museum describes that, 'the ruining of the medieval city also presented new opportunities for imagining a novel urban infrastructure and design ... a brilliant new London would emerge phoenix-like from the flames.'[37] I reviewed several official explainers of the fire and all point out, a little too enthusiastically perhaps, the role of the fire in making London even better than it was before.

The 'Build Back Better' narrative, the BBB as it is known in disaster response, is one that I know very well. It even became a jarring mantra for a time, used by consultants involved in environmental recovery, between about 2004 and 2010. Its official origins are said to be found in speeches by Bill Clinton, former US president, to the UN about recovering from the 2004 tsunami. It was finally rendered passé in the years after the pandemic when its repeated use by US President Joe Biden in speeches and policies led to weariness and criticism.

The last lesson I want to end with definitely belongs to Dad. It is the saying that by hammer and hand do all things stand. The mantra of the blacksmith and the woodturner. That what comes next is not just built, but first imagined and then quarried and then slowly reborn.

There is a rebuild that comes next, not the management-speak of the three Bs, but something softer and slower. It is up to all of us to be the custodians and the creators of it. Every aftermath begins with the laying down of a single brick and a scrape of mortar. It involves the learning of new skills and the going to uncomfortable places. That's true of every single thing we will ever face. It is time to craft.

Looking backwards to move forwards

During the pandemic, I got to know some of the custodians of the National Covid Memorial Wall. A 500-metre-long stretch of wall along the South Bank of the River Thames, it stands, significantly, opposite the Palace of

Westminster, where Parliament is housed. Starting in March 2021, the families of those who had died from coronavirus began to paint small red hearts on it, unauthorised. Defiant and naughty. They wanted politicians to have to look upon it as they made their decisions. The red hearts were often accompanied by a name or message written in marker pen. The 'custodians of the wall' were painting onto something definitely built to last, but their own mode of adding to it was fragile and scratchy. In their lighter moments, their survivance in the face of bereavement, they would talk to me about the trial and error that went into finding the right and most durable red paint. I also noticed something else about the work. The labour had a point. It was important that their backs ached as they stood there and coloured. That they got wet in the rain. That they had to start all over again when the colour ran. The work was part of the survivance.

Through their admirable stubbornness and the eventual sourcing of the right red paint-pens, they created one of the most impressive memorials I have ever seen. With none of the official wrangling, lengthy procurements and appointment of architects that usually go with the process. Research suggests that pandemics are particularly problematic to memorialise – being both everywhere and nowhere – but somehow they had managed it.

They recolour the hearts regularly. They are artists taking great care over the consistency and the lines. If you can't get there yourself to paint a heart, you can request a dedication and they will add it for you and send you a photo. At first, the custodians were told clearly that the wall could not last and that after a few weeks of indulgence, the hearts would be washed off. I very much doubt that will happen now, years later. It would be like taking a pressure hose to a Monet. They made this and it stays.

For certain types of losses, a key step of the big build is the memorial. That is the first time that we get to do our crafting. Something needs to be put onto and into the world to show what has been. The act of making it is always important to me. Memorials are often hewn from stone or metal. Wood and trees also feature heavily too. Something that will endure. The process of getting to memorialisation is a book in itself but many aspects of this fascinate me.[38]

My aunty Deb, a no-nonsense charter sailor of yachts around the Caribbean and handler of global banking risks, took charge of our family slump last year by commissioning a tree and a seat for my dad that sits in my garden. Suddenly, there was a place to go when things felt overwhelming. My children decorated it with wooden hearts and Tom planted daffodils at the base. But Dad was very easy to memorialise because he is everywhere. The nature of the help that he liked to constantly offer, combined with the craftsman that he was, means that he is immortalised in all sorts of wonderful places. I get to lay my hand where his hands worked on the lathe several times a month. Friends' bathrooms or bookcases. The wooden gates of a local playgroup. The doors of a church.

Benches made in life so they did not need to be commissioned in death. He also did something else. He was generous with his skills and passed them on along with his tools to both of his sons-in-law. Now, there are Dad-inspired windowsills and doorframes and playhouses, made by the sorcerer's apprentices. His favourite wood was big strong oak. The wood that frames many a fine building. In the same way that people tell you to take your shoes off and crunkle your bare feet into grass to de-stress and connect with nature, Dad would see whether he had some oak to plane.

It always interests me that we do something so similar at home to what we do in big disaster response. After a period of illness, people will often have a big spring clean. Throw lots of things out and have a jolly good dust. Sometimes, within hours of the death of a person from illness, the family will often want to dispose of not the person's things but the effects that remind them of their decline. The spectacles and the clothes will stay but they will immediately want to bag up the pills, the ointments, the food replacement drinks and the waterproof bed mats. One of the first things they ask for, even before the funeral is organised, is for the special hospital bed arranged with the local palliative care team to be gone. They clear their own personal disaster scene in the same way that we do as responders. Their tools are big black bin bags and cloths, and a grateful charity shop; ours are tents and cranes and delivery trucks.

Alongside the clearing out should come the gratitude. Nothing gets done, there is no forward motion, without a decent thank you to each other and also to yourself. The further we move into adulthood, the more we forget how to praise or affirm ourselves. Every single response that I walk into I start with a thank you to the responders – thanks for being here today, thank you for giving me this time. Thank you for what you are doing for these people who have no idea that you are even doing this work because it is hidden. I always meet a little bit of resistance when I suggest that people might want to take that thank you home and say it loudly to kin. Emerging from the slump can leave us bitter and introspective. We can blind ourselves to the help we have had from those closest to us. But gratitude is plant food. Use it liberally. When looking at the Covid Memorial Wall, it is hard not to notice that our leaders, globally, appear to have almost completely bypassed the gratitude stage of the big build.

When I go somewhere, I have learned to scour for past disaster patinas and sometimes they are exceptionally well hidden. I have also realised that my own view of whether a place has 'recovered' is skewed by the way I catalogue and remember disaster in my brain. I record the placenames on a cerebral rolodex. When I see them on a road sign they fizz and sting. Dunblane, Überlingen, Waco, Hiroshima, Chernobyl, Hillsborough, Lockerbie, Gresford. But that's not what everyone does – not everyone is visiting the blue plaque or looking for the line that the water reached on the wall. Over time, they fade a little. Eventually, you can only see them when you know where to look. You never lose the scarring, and nor would you want to, but around the thirty-to-forty-year mark, I have learned that the scars become less livid and more just part of the place.

But every crisis, every disaster, every place will need its own memorial and a home for its stories. The best are crafted carefully but not too slowly, as that leaves a community in limbo.

In the years after 11 September, I kept in touch with colleagues working on the management of the Ground Zero site, the national memorial park for Flight 93 and the rebuild of the Pentagon (for obvious reasons, this latter site was rebuilt under a veil of secrecy). The build can feel too quick for some, too brazen. Manhattan after the attacks on 11 September 2001 was always going to come back from its disaster in some form, but some decisions can feel way too soon and too bold. One such controversy was the decisions around what should happen to the World Trade Center site. Architects and consultants will claim to place 'families at the heart' of a rebuild but it can be easy to forget the pain of the bereaved. Somebody gets to decide that it is time to survive. Others may not be there yet. One thing that we often struggle to get right after disaster is recognising that there are different losses, different people, different circumstances all caused by the same one tragedy. Responders try desperately to homogenise them.

The pace at Ground Zero was relentless. It was an entanglement of body fragment recovery and rubble clearance, but always with one weather eye on what the future might look like. Ideas, tolerances were tested.

Lights were beamed into the sky to the same height as the towers in the years immediately after the attacks. Gently, ideas for what would be built back were explored and tested. There was an incredibly difficult balance to be struck in that whatever was built also had to provide a resting place for the thousands of tiny fragments of human tissue that were recovered from the scene but were unidentifiable. In addition to this, it would need to take its place in Manhattan alongside many other places.

Over time, the site transformed from piles and piles of debris, suffocating dust, human remains and jagged girders. When I visited in 2007, it had been smoothed out and resembled the staging for a new motorway. The site finally opened in 2014 as both a memorial and a museum. The two cavernous footings of the original World Trade Center towers are now pools of water, surrounded by carved names of all those who died.

The decision was taken that this location would need to do something else to answer to a human need. It would educate others about what has gone before. This became the museum within the 9/11 memorial. I have visited the museum several times and personally struggle with an event that feels so now and raw as well as historic, but I also tell myself that it's always been like that. The new generations have always needed to archive what went before.

Our need to mark the moment when the bad stars hit is often only partially understood but it manifests in many different ways. I love how so many people after difficult times get a tattoo. Many survivors I know, often previously uninked, will roll up a sleeve or a trouser leg at a one-year anniversary to quietly show me a tiny, beautiful iconograph of the day or the loss. It is something that I often see in bereavement. One friend has the *Great Wave off Kanagawa*, the iconic image of tsunami, tattooed down the inside of her arm so that she never forgets the first wave of the coronavirus pandemic and what was asked of her. I remain determined to have an Estwing hammer inked on my forearm in permanent memory of my dad, if only I can work out a way to sneak it past my mum.

Ninety years on, they build and they craft in Wrexham too. New shops have opened. The council can't keep up with the need for new taxi licences to keep up with demand as people travel to football matches from all around the world. The club's sponsors are now some of the world's best-known brands. The pub made famous in the documentary, The Turf, has expanded and made room for thousands of new visitors. Tickets to actual matches are like hen's teeth. Ambitious plans for a new stand have been submitted to the council. Some things still stand. St Giles' church still stands tall on the hill watching over these new developments, the place where Mum and Dad were married. Dad in trousers that were too long and over-dusted the tops of his shoes. There are plans to build a new conference centre and hotel, with support of a £25 million grant from the Welsh government. And a promise to position the old pit wheel at the heart of it all.

In the end, the point of all this is often not the memorial itself, but the act of making it. It is the physical manifestation of the story we are telling ourselves about the event. And those stories are important because they are tools for healing, moving us gently into a future.

Sometimes, we are even helped in this by nature. When I started out in my career, you learned never to speak about the otters. There was many a seasoned emergency planner still muttering about the camera-pulling power of those otters.

Just after 5am on Tuesday 5 January 1993, a Liberian-registered tanker, *The Braer*, ran aground at Garths Ness, Shetland Islands, a place of spectacular natural beauty and environmental importance, where people lived and fished. The cargo, all 84,700 tonnes of crude oil, spilled into the sea and onto the rocks. Fossil fuels, spilled or burned or mined for, have been a bedrock of so many of my disaster experiences. The role of fuel in so many incidents to which I have responded means that I have learned something about their qualities – their heaviness, their components, their ability to burn at cremation temperatures.

For many evenings that winter, the news across the United Kingdom was filled with images of almost 2,000 dead seabirds and desperate attempts to wash the thick crude oil off the feathers of others with a chance of survival. Twenty-nine seals and three otters also died, and the images of the attempts to save otters became one of those totemic images of the incident. The public made donations to help them and were agog for otter progress reports. Later on in the 1990s, when people died in other UK disasters, it would be muttered that they still didn't get the same attention as the wildlife of the Shetland Islands had. Even a decade after *The Braer*, seasoned responders would still bark at newcomers: 'Do not get me started on those bloody otters!' Which took some explanation.

But one thing that nature did on the night *The Braer* ran aground will stay with me. The crude formed an airborne spray that was carried on the storm-force winds, which was described in the official aftermath report as a 'distinctive and surprising feature of the incident'. Later analysis would suggest that the strong mechanical action of the waves that night more effectively broke up the crude than anything a human response could do (although the incident remained incredibly serious).

I never stop being impressed when the natural world steps in to play its part in the big build. It deserves its own tabard in the response. When the special bacteria brought in to eat up an oil spill works faster than anyone predicted or when the rain and the sea spray work together to stop the crude spilling as far as it might. I often wonder if people might sleep better if they knew how many times the natural world actually collaborates with emergency planners and not against them. The times that the wind suddenly changes and moves the fire in the direction of the river rather than the town. The times that the river does not quite flood.

Exodus or epiphany

At the end, it is time to look to the future.

There were reports of two types of long-term behaviour in survivors of the World Trade Center towers. Something similar was present in research from earlier disasters and it will be familiar to many of us. I started to call these two categories the Great Exodus and the Great Epiphany. They have been present in the subtext in every life event I have ever seen, big or small.

People often dramatically make a life change: they decide they cannot do their job; they leave their marriage; or they pack up, try to sell their house. They often make these decisions in a way that is quite self-destructive, sudden and poorly thought-through. They just scarper – the Great Exodus. These people often become very bitter and dissatisfied. The feelings were natural but the execution is – often because of a lack of support – awry.

But I have learned that, given the right support and resources, there is a way to channel those feelings into something else. This is what I call the Great Epiphany. The Epiphany feels more measured, solid and better thought-through. People do still quit their jobs, but with a plan. They leave a job they hate for the one they always dreamed of doing. They take time to sell the city flat and draw up a travel itinerary. Or they invest on a smaller scale – in self-care, in their mental health. In getting the dog they had always wanted. Rediscovering a passion for craft and the outside world is often a big part of the epiphany. This very much fits with the self-actualisation part of Maslow's pyramid as people look again at what is important to them after a period of burnout and self-questioning. They seek a new balance between purpose and fulfilment.

Most of us need a helping hand to bring on epiphanies. The art therapists who work at the Henry Dickens centre see adults as well as children. It has been a great privilege to learn from them about the ways that people engage with making art during extremis. Adults doing art therapy often draw what they really want, where they want to be, and this stimulates a discussion of what is stopping them from getting it.

Hospitals also have started to open up art therapy groups for their workers, much more so since the pandemic, as part of a wellbeing package from a health employer desperately trying to stem a haemorrhaging workforce. Those therapists tell me that the first few times the reluctant nurses or doctors engage with art therapy, they may be late or stay only for ten minutes. Some say they 'don't do art'. They may fidget with the materials or check their phone. But eventually, they start to engage. Sometimes the pictures may be big angry strokes of a sharp pen that pierces the paper or angry dots. Rainbows referencing those that were everywhere in the first lockdown, but with expletives written within in tiny lettering. They may tear it up at the end of the hour. But slowly, something begins to emerge. Many of the participants go on to sign up for more sessions. Later, some apply for different roles in healthcare or have signed up to be retrained in a slightly different role.

The Great Epiphany is also about a movement and redirection of energy. The energy of afterwards, potentially destructive but also potentially propelling, is best when channelled towards the horizon. When it finally appears from the post-disaster clouds, you have to create subtle shift in energies to take you towards it. You have to start laying down the bricks to get there. That's the only way to initiate the moment for great realisation that differentiates epiphany from exodus. Exodus is throwing everything up in the air without a good plan.

This difference (as between hope and hopium) is often linked to a robust analysis of what sits behind it. It starts with looking at the evidence base and interrogating whether something is realistic. If you are supporting someone who is considering a major life change and you are not sure whether its exodus or epiphany, it can be useful to evaluate the way in which they describe the planned change. If it is being framed as an escape, getting ready to walk out, the last resort, fuelled with anger and nihilism, it is probably an exodus.

On the ground

In my first book, I wrote about Tom's diagnosis of chronic disease and the impact on his career and his life. The question I have been asked most frequently when I have been speaking to people about the book is not about the big disasters I included within it, but this one, the one that is closest to home. Did Tom ever get to fly again? The answer is that he will never fly again, and will always have to manage a life before and a life after. We have lived alongside the chaos and the uncertainty of rapid change. The impact assessment that I made for my own family when our world folded in was honest and bleak, and it involved saying things out loud that made the man I love look like he had been punched. *You will not fly again.*

But my life in disaster steeled me as to why I was doing it. There was no time for hopium. Our reasonable worst-case scenario, the loss of the life before, was definitely here. We ticked several of the Holmes and Rahe scale all at once. I wanted to build back, but first of all we had to say what this had done. The Civil Aviation Authority removed Tom's licence to fly. I feared it would be ceremoniously brutal, sent back to him cut into tiny pieces or some similar cruelty. But it was just an email. That he would fly again was now hopium. But we could keep hope that there would be something else. We could lay down the first brick.

When writing this chapter, I ambushed Tom over his cereal and asked what things help the most with his rebuild. He chuckled and said, 'Am I supposed to say you?!' But he does admit that me being able to see a horizon and an afterwards slowly helped. He allows me a tiny bit of credit for my advice to him that in order to get to the epiphany stage you have to have made a series of difficult decisions. It's a particular type of decisiveness that is required in bad times when choosing not between good options but between several bad ones.

There was a road towards a great exodus, one where he checked out physically and emotionally, and he stumbled down it for a while. He talks gently and quietly to my mum now about trying to see a way through when everything is ripped from under you.

Tom's illness means he has to pace carefully and if he is feeling particularly unwell all he can do is rest. But he has found a rebuild. Doing things, making things, creating things is what comes next for him. He has learned about working with wood and concrete. Skills that he can get lost in, use his hands, use the precision that made him an airline pilot. Measure twice, cut once, as a good carpenter will always caution.

He has laid down literal bricks and mortar. And he has filled the cupboard that also houses his flight log books with medals from the half marathons that have also become his passion. He will never not miss it, not ache for the flying. But he is building something new now too.

The afterwards

I smile wryly at the tales of London's rebuild post 1666. The wrangles. The delays. The familiarity of the tale of a fallout between the fellows of the Royal Society, overseeing the plans, when Christopher Wren presented his ideas to the king before anybody else had had a chance to see them. Maybe he thought they would steal his ideas or veto them. Some things never change.

I also marvel at the timescale – fifty years for the majority of the rebuild, which seems rapid and impressive. Some ideas like a whole new city grid system were vetoed and the streets were built back as they were. I get this. I have seen many places do just that. In 2025, it is not yet Amatrice's turn. A post-pandemic crisis budget and the imposition of strict EU funding rules has seen their building recovery budget stripped to almost nothing. Almost a decade on, half of Amatrice's homes are yet to be fully repaired and no work has started on its churches. A wasteland remains: 'Windowless shells of old apartment blocks haunt the immediate outskirts . . . residents of the old town still live in emergency prefabs built right after the earthquake. Much of the town's ecosystem of life and commerce has been remade in tacky newbuilds along the flanks of a mountain freeway.'[39]

Jersey waits for its turn too but the pace seems quicker there and its hoped that new houses and a memorial park will be built in the next few years. Gresford's has begun again, the tragedy frozen in time, the rebuild one hundred years delayed, partially funded and inspired from across an ocean.

Although some of the braver designs were vetoed in London in 1666, the influence of the new thinking is said to have transformed the city's architecture significantly in the coming decades. There is a difficult truth about the innovation that can come out of disaster, a positive that we never know quite how to describe and which I am deeply uncomfortable with. Disasters can bring forward changes that were expected to take decades, but it should not need such pain and tragedy to bring them. I remember listening to an official in the pandemic describe how the rapid switch to online methods of delivering teaching had swept in technology changes in weeks that they thought might take twenty years. There were many downsides to the way we approached schooling and children's needs in the pandemic – an online learning package is not the same as school – but I can see where some innovations have helped. Extremis innovates. The medical care we give to people injured now in road traffic collisions and bomb attacks has been transformed by the learning from conflicts in Iraq and Afghanistan. But you still wish the war had never been.

Perhaps counterintuitively, I think the more that the shrinking world changes and fills, the more building and rebuilding we will have to do. A future with brave recovery leaders would see buildings repurposed and refurbished. Energy would be harnessed differently. Houses would be built as homes not as unsafe vessels for somebody else's profit.

We have the right to demand more from government and policy makers, to ask for leaders who are schooled and skilled in the work of disaster recovery, who understand what the pandemic did. So much of the onus is on us, as individuals, as communities, in the aftermath. There are things no one else can do for us. And we have seen the sort of mistakes that are made and the further hurt that is inflicted when decisions are wrongfully taken out of the hands of those who are impacted by them, stripping their dignity. But there are essential things that will always be the responsibility of governments. We should all have access to ways that we can thrive. People deserve apprenticeships and training schemes. We see a greater demand for access to parks and to want to get outside following pandemics and people taking up sports. This need must be filled. The research also suggested that more people consider moving into healthcare and social care professions after a crisis such as the Covid-19 pandemic, but I think that, sadly, we might buck that particular trend for a while. There may be little appeal for some time in working in sectors that are under-resourced and undervalued.

I was asked to give an evening talk to beleaguered healthcare workers in Manchester Monastery – a building that is truly one of the most magnificent examples of architectural survival I have ever seen. I could not have been scaffolded better for a talk on the disaster recovery graph – the slump and the uptick.

I had only checked the location on a digital map and had not really paid much attention to the building's own journey of recovery. But when I snuck off to fine-tune my talk in a dark corridor, I found myself surrounded by floor-to-ceiling wall charts that detailed the monastery's descent into complete dereliction over twenty years. The lead from the roof was sold off, the altars collapsed into the rain-threatened naves. The statues of saints were taken to Sotheby's and sold off as garden furniture. Nobody is quite sure what happened to the Wadsworth organ that sent sound up to heaven, but it is believed that it was sold off for scrap. By 1996, the building – begun in 1866 – was completely derelict. And yet somehow, it was brought back from the dead. A couple, Paul and Elaine Griffiths, bought the structure for the sum of a pound and then started a fundraising campaign. Each piece was slowly revived and what stands there now is truly remarkable. And a testament to the power of the hammer and the hand.

I have learned that life after any sort of turbulence asks so much of us. It asks us to assess constantly our ethical framework and think honestly about whether something is achievable. It asks us to take positives or innovations from situations that should never have been allowed to happen. It asks us to simultaneously remember, forget, memorialise and move on, all in one, painful breath. It asks us to remember that it too shall pass while simultaneously holding on to the idea that it is the greatest thing you might ever do. Your thinking has to be both little and big. There are ways in which thinking like this might change the world. But there are also certainly ways it might help you do things differently *just for you*. The two are equally important. Your own rebuild is as important as anything else.

Build you back first.

Your recovery kit

Start any new build, literal or metaphorical, with a thank you.
I always think of this as like a little Ritual of Land Acknowledgement made to show respect for Indigenous occupants of a place, as this thank you

honours what has gone before and the sacrifices that were made. Thank at home and at work.

Use a daily routine.
Tom says that he found a routine really helpful. He runs at a set time and in all weathers and he sets himself challenges. Competitive events in the calendar become targets. In the aftermath of his diagnosis, I was ruthless on making him get up, get dressed and showered. Sometimes he did not buy into it, or want to believe it, but he could see what I was trying to do in emphasising that all his other roles – spouse, home builder, Labrador trainer and, most especially, father – each had a value too. Make sure the people in your life know they are needed. Say it more often and louder than feels necessary or British! Tom resisted all my attempts to make him volunteer formally, but I have noticed that he has very subtly become a vital figure in supporting male friends with mental and physical issues. Helping others can take many forms.

Evaluate epiphany or exodus.
I see a lot of decision-making in my work, occasionally done well and often done badly. Our bodies, our guts and our instincts point us to one answer but our egos or fear of upsetting those around us may point us to another. I think the adage that the first decision you come to is often the right one has a lot of merit, but don't make big decisions when

you are distressed or under the influence of drugs or alcohol. Do you have a plan? Is it moving you towards a new horizon or simply throwing everything up in the air?

Stay flexible.
The best plans are flexible. I actually think this is one thing we have got much better at since the pandemic: people are becoming used to adapting to disappointment or sudden change. Talk out loud about plan Bs and alternative arrangements.

Consume bad news differently.
Try to limit and visualise placing the concerns it may bring into an archive box and focusing in, really shrinking down, to what you can control. I always visualise tying that box with a big bow, even though it may still rattle a little bit, as if there is a gremlin inside it.

Local news is where local planning teams will feed the updates to. In case of a crisis where you live, it is worth tuning into them. Set aside time to read news online and then that's it for the day. If you find yourself becoming anxious while absorbing news, move very deliberately onto another task or go outside.

Dispense with negative comparisons.
Completely. Take them out of your mouth. You might be feeling that your rebuild is slower than

somebody else's or your path is less worthy. I literally erupt when somebody around me starts to place less value on themselves than someone else. You are worthy. Your path is just fine.

Heal together.
Learn about how to walk on the path to the build with other people and read about how other people have travelled it. You can't just stumble blindly; you have to see something to work towards. Actively seek out activities that might bring you and some friends 'silly joy' – I would have been lost without the cinema and theatre trips and the tears shed in coffee shops that helped me to see the path.

End Note
Whatever Next

'Life is a preparation for the fullest enjoyment of the next minute, but to be aware of death is to appreciate the never-to-come-again worth of that minute, free of the dark.'[40]

Life changed forever in April 2023 when I lost my dad. My dad was a great big Ent, the tree-like beings of Tolkien's Middle Earth known for their strength and their presence and the way that they think. There is only a before and an after without him. People die and then there is a hole that never fills. I think we need to be more comfortable and less confronted by the idea that the loss never gets any smaller. It is just there. It wasn't his style to want to be immortalised in a book but he would have liked the idea very much that people right now have some help. He always thought people were great and he could almost always find some common ground or something good in them. He had no sense of an inner circle – everyone was his neighbour and his kin.

I think he knew that he wouldn't make old bones, and although he was desperately sad at the thought of leaving my mum, I honestly think he was OK with that. People forget now, and need to forget now, that in spring 2020, none of us knew how long we had. Some of us did not make it. My dad had received a letter from the health secretary, facsimile signature, reminding him that he was 'clinically extremely vulnerable' and telling him to stay inside. By then, with a planner's weather eye I had already moved him and Mum in with us.

Dad and I would sneak off to the garage, while food was cooked and children read to, and talk about what next. I would spend all day being a grown-up and a planner, a lantern bearer, telling others about how to get ready. But with him, finally, I could admit I was scared. He would remind me that there was nothing to be afraid of. We were together. We had right now. And that living has always been done in the gaps. The idea that there has ever been anything other than living in the gaps was a fallacy we tell each other to get to sleep.

His mum, my gran, had this wonderful habit of shaking her head with mock exasperation at whatever antic her children, grandchildren and then eventually great grandchildren had got up to and saying 'whatever next' with great flourish. I loved it as an expression. I saw the enquiry within the statement. What *was* next I wondered, from the earliest age. I took the next stage apart, piece by piece. And later on, I would find others who take great comfort in doing the same. It's a scary question but such a helpful one too.

Gran Lucy knew that the answers to that question could be infinite and dark. Born under the looming clouds that led to the First World War in early 1913, she was a fervent learner with a particular love of Latin and Ancient Greek. She played lacrosse for the county. But then her life, and so many others, was turned upside down. Her brief typewritten notes reflecting on the early days of the Second World War capture her shock when war was declared on 3 September 1939. A few days later, she found herself in a long queue at a registry office to get married. She wrote that she and my grandfather had said they would marry if war broke out and it had, so there they were. The queue was full of other young, frightened couples doing the same.

I sometimes wonder about the rapidity and the laser-sharp certainty of that decision-making and how it's especially honed in times of crisis. Our bodies are trained to focus down to the tightest of peripheries; our pupils literally shrink in. We focus in in a way that modern life rarely asks us to and are able to see with a different sort of clarity. You think harder and faster than at any other time. Every night could be your last night.

She taught in a school in the daytime as the bombs fell. She had been nervous about whether the headmaster would allow her to carry on, as the convention was not to continue to employ married women. But most of the other young women had hastily married too, she wrote, and he was left with no choice. In the evening, they cooked meals for the dockyard workers. She trained in air raid precaution and was responsible for sounding the sirens. For letting people know with as much warning as she possibly could of what was ahead. She worked alongside the tin-hatted wardens and in her notes remarked on their strictness. 'They would be very firm with those who neglected their blackout. Not a light must show.' But eventually, it would be their jobs to lead their frightened neighbours back out into the wreckage, bearing a lantern.

Grandma Lucy could be a stern woman with exacting standards, but I always noted that she did something that I also do – she savoured. She took time with a piece of apple pie, in case it was the last slice she ever had. She would clasp her hands together with delight and do a little stim at something mundane yet also wonderful – cress seedlings on a paper towel, a gifted box of toffees, a new cardigan, a new grandchild. Each a precious wonder that counteracts the darkness over there. Sometimes, when life is too comfortable, we forget the precious.

Dad took 'whatever next' to the next level. He would say out loud where the path might go, including the darker tributaries. It is behaviour that his daughter turned into a career and a practice he shared with soldiers in elite units around the world. There is a particular technique in the Special Forces world that involves talking out loud about each stage of the most likely trajectory of a worst-case scenario. If they are going to be captured and tortured, what that might look like, how this will all come to an end. They air their own demise and then they step into it, cores rigid and minds set. This technique of spelling out the worst can be an anathema in other places and settings, but I have come to understand that it can be an essential tool. I think back to talking with Bex over our pancakes and how we believe fully in the motto of the No 1 Parachute Training School RAF that 'Knowledge Dispels Fear'.

The world is changing around us, just like it has always done. If we are going to live alongside 'permacrisis', what does that look and feel like? Many of us have begun to question whether recovery, or even recovering, of a place or its people is possible. But I think we keep the faith in the value of a plan for both before and for after. A plan doesn't have to be rigid, it can be a conversation, a hymn even, that tells us what principles to follow. And then I think back to Dad and I in the garage, sat under strip lighting with a mug of tea, when he told me about what would come next. People were going to need people more than ever. There would be great uncertainty and more conflict, truths muddied, help slow to come.

Many people around the world live with intense precarity every single day and often are the best preppers. For everything that comes next, we will need every single lesson in this book and so many more. One of the many gifts that this work has given me is a chance to share lessons and practices internationally. It has also shown me how wrong we get it sometimes. Our ways of living alongside disaster are not working. We will need to rethink our relationship with place and with resources and with each other. We have to stop shouting at each other and using fear as a big stick. We have to do something truly difficult – both live in the now and prep for the winter. Everyone will have to be our neighbour.

One of the last conversations Dad and I had involved me chastising him lightly that he had not prepared me very well for my working world, where people can be cruel or thoughtless. He didn't understand not caring about something or not taking an interest. He couldn't bear the thought of not being humane. It was only when I went out into the world that I realised how rare his qualities were. He never really understood or would accept what a genuine treasure he was – so kind, frustratingly generous. As his daughters, we were sometimes a little anxious about how much he would do or give away. Always paying for the young mum in front in the queue whose debit card was declined while everyone else tutted. So consistent – such an underrated virtue – just always there, no false promises, humble, so loving, so ready to help. And he was so gentle, which is also not really understood by the world as an attribute. So patient, even when in pain, and such a great listener. He was a gentle helper, a passionate believer that it would all work out in the end. And most importantly of all, he believed it all mattered, this all mattered, and was worth the effort.

Life is uncertain. What comes next is uncertain. But knowing that sharpens the mind into narrow focus. My biggest lesson of all, relearned once again, these last two years? That there is no guarantee of tomorrow. All you ever have is today. Be acutely aware of the time limits placed on you and allow that to focus you. Trust me that minutes are precious. There is no other way to live now but alongside the uncertainty, and with great delight.

Acknowledgements

First rule of Acknowledgements Club is that if I said thank you in *When The Dust Settles* they apply equally as robustly now. You are all my support crew.

There has been no better home, yet again, for a book than Hodder & Stoughton and I am indebted to Kirty Topiwala, Rebecca Mundy, Anna Baty, Kate Miles, Lucy Buxton, Olivia French and Dominic Gribben.

Thank you to Chad Worsley and Ben Dempsey Sawin for the audiobook.

At JULA, my thanks to Jo Unwin, Nisha Bailey, Daisy Arendell and Donna Greaves.

Celia Hayley – no words for how grateful I am for your wisdom and perseverance.

A grateful shout out to the children of the Henry Dickens Centre and to all those who make it so special but particular thanks to Anne, Kayla, Casey, Faye, Jack, Holly, Lucy and Susan. And an extra shout out to Stanley!

Aunty Cal, Uncle Mike, Matt, Jen, Phil, Freddie and Daisy – keep hitting those sales targets for me. Love you all.

To all the chaps but particular thanks to Ed, Loui, Steve, Plip, Adi, Jock, Mark, John, Joe, Paul, Snash and Jules. See you around the campfire soon.

Janet and the Levitt/ Myers crew – thank you for being there in the darkest of hours. Payne and Myers Clan – anything is possible when you are around. Peter, thank you for rushing to our aid. Aunty Vivian, Rachel Leah and Amanda Coleman – for the footprints and the lanterns. Johns' Boys Male Chorus for a soundtrack to lift us up and particular thanks to Mr Aron Cook.

To Jen, Alex, Luke and Nelly – we would have been completely lost without the love and the laughs and the paté.

Julia Wheeler, Caroline Sanderson, Caroline Lang – you made me feel like a writer and chatting to you all again was what I thought of when the writing got really hard. To Carrie at Booka – 'just write it' proved to be surprisingly helpful advice.

Annalisa Barbieri and Philippa Perry – the very best recovery advisers in the universe.

Mr P – thank you for being the co-creator of the concept of Twinergy.

For getting this one done, special thanks to Nick and Kate Easthope, Dr Mark Roberts, Benjamin Roberts, Nicky Young, Alison Anderson, Helen Hinds, Dr Helen Turner, Matthew Hogan, Nathan Hazlehurst, Hannagh Calpin, Chris McConigall and Ted, Rob Grayston, Mary Mullix, Anna Griffiths, Elizabeth Turner, Elmarie Marais, Dr Kandida Purnell, Professor Jenny Edkins, Dr Amy Cortvriend, Professor Flora Cornish, Cathy Long, Caroline,

Acknowledgements

Tom C and R, Jane, Elizabeth Greenwood, Eileen Tully, Dr Caroline McMullan, Dr Anne Eyre, Jelena Watkins, Emma Dodgson, Arthur, Frank, Adrian, Mike R, Mike and Susan Greenwood, Jolie Wills, Elizabeth McNaughton, Professor Tracy Daszkiewicz, Professor Catherine Mason, Dr James Adeley, Hannah, James, Debbie, Professor Lucina Hackman, Dr Hugh Deeming, the Barlow family, the Carpenter family, John Pitchers, Leanne Hunt, Chathura Malalasena, Jane and Beccy, Sara Lloyd-Thomas, my Wallasey girls, Sahina Bibi, Nigel and Michael, Dr Sian Williams, Deb, Amber, James and Rosie, Professor Lady Sue Black, Professor Phil Scraton, Jen Williams, Uncle Dave and the tribe, Aunty Ros, Uncle Phil and families, Barb Gillman, Dr Meredith Tise and all at the Centre for Death and Society, University of Bath. And a lifetime of gratitude to the truly marvellous Dr Lesley Perman-Kerr.

To the Pritchett family and their indomitable Bex – love always.

Professor John Troyer, for everything and for the best article ever written on grief.

Sam Knight, for the profile and for my most treasured possession, my Dad's words.

To Luke Wright, thank you for giving my Mum the first belly laughs after the terrible night. Your verses are pure, dirty magic.

Dr Stephanie deGiorgio – thank you for all your solidarity, support and bloody good advice on lives with chronic illness.

Dr Emily Cooper and family – your bravery in these horrible times has changed the world.

Dr Gemma Ahearne, I am in awe of you. Thank you for helping me find the words for holding more than one truth. You make everything make sense.

To Clare, Rick, Austin and Emmy – we walk this path together always.

Where would I be without the sense making and true joy of Erin, Megan, Sam, Jude and Emma. I give thanks for you every day.

To Kit, bouncing, timely proof that good things continue to happen. Thank you for bringing the light.

To my Mum – love you Nanabags, the Nandini, the Naan Bread – I know you hate every minute of bereavement bootcamp but he would be so, so very proud of you.

Elizabeth and Mabel – you will always be the point of it all.

Tom Easthope – thank you for letting me share you with the world *again*.

And the final acknowledgement of all belongs to Bob Payne. Thank you for being our Dad.

Further Reading

I hope that this book has given you some support and guidance in coping with crisis. For further reading, I include all of my articles and podcasts on my website www.whatevernext.info. I also really recommend the following books which have seen me through difficult times and taught me important things.

Recovery: The Lost Art of Convalescence by Dr Gavin Francis (Wellcome Collection, 2022) is essential on re-thinking your own approach to the lost art of convalescence. I gift it to everyone I know who is unwell or about to have surgery.

The Gift of Fear: Survival Signals That Protect Us from Violence by Gavin de Becker (Bloomsbury, 2000) is one I use for thinking about intuition and personal safety, as well as *Safe: How to Stay Safe in a Dangerous World* by Chris Ryan (Coronet, 2017).

Rise: A First-aid Kit for Getting Through Tough Times by Sian Williams (Orion, 2016) is a beautiful companion when facing the life changes that cancer treatment brings.

When It Is Darkest: Why People Die by Suicide and What We Can Do to Prevent It by Rory O'Connor (Vermilion, 2021) is a powerful and necessary book about why people die by suicide.

Grief Works: Stories of Life, Death and Surviving by Julia Samuel (Penguin Life, 2021) has helped me and Mum, particularly when it felt like we might be getting it wrong. We also both got a lot of comfort from Jill Halfpenny's memoir *A Life Reimagined: My Journey of Hope in the Midst of Loss* (Macmillan, 2024).

How to Feel Better: A Guide to Navigating the Ebb and Flow of Life by Cathy Rentzenbrink (Bluebird, 2023) is great on what not to say to people who might be struggling and how to think more about ways to help.

The Way We Survive: Notes on Rape Culture by Catriona Morton (Trapeze, 2021) is a difficult, important read on the aftermath of sexual assault and is insightful on how to help yourself and also how to help those who confide in you.

For thinking about coming back as a community I find Rebecca Solnit's writing in *Hope in the Dark: Untold Histories, Wild Possibilities* (Canongate, 2024) and *A Paradise Built from Hell: The Extraordinary Communities That Arise in Disaster* (Viking, 2009) incredibly powerful.

Jack Saul's *Collective Trauma, Collective Healing: Promoting Community Resilience in the Aftermath of Disaster* (Routledge, 2022) reminds us that any recovering process is built on sustained and trusted relationships.

For thinking about how to empower children I found Myleene Klass's book *They Don't Teach This at School:*

Essential Knowledge to Tackle Everyday Challenges (HQ, 2022) about essential knowledge for children tackling challenges, practical and social, really helpful here. For understanding more about supporting adolescents, I use Lucy Foulkes' *Coming of Age* (Penguin, 2024).

Wintering: The Power of Rest and Retreat in Difficult Times by Katherine May (Rider, 2020) is a great help for thinking about seasonality, rest and fallow periods.

As a new parent I also found Ruby's Wax's writing on mindfulness for parents, babies and children in *A Mindfulness Guide for the Frazzled* (Penguin Life, 2016), very helpful. As Ruby suggests, I would regulate my breathing to the baby's and then we would look directly at each other. Even now that she is a lot bigger, I find my younger daughter can be calmed by holding her to my heart – particularly heart to heart.

I found *The Curse of Lovely: How to Break Free from the Demands of Others and Learn How to Say No* by Jacqui Marson (Piatkus, 2013) helpful on thinking about ways we might be editing out our own needs and becoming worn down by going along with the needs of others. She advocates thinking about all the times when you might be leaving out your own feelings.

For thinking about the changing climate and what it means for disaster management, I use *Disasterology: Dispatches from the Frontlines of the Climate Crisis* by Samantha Montano (Park Row, 2021).

I have taken great comfort from Gaia Vince's work *Nomad Century: How to Survive the Climate Upheaval* (Allen Lane, 2023). Gaia takes inevitable global heating as a foundation to her work. She paints a bleak but necessary picture of the incremental changes that will continue in our world, particularly in a zone around the equator. People will move about a lot more, and Gaia challenges the framing of this as a problem or a threat.

For learning about listening better, I use Kathyrn Mannix's book *Listen: How to Find the Words for Tender Conversations* (William Collins, 2021).

Dear Life: A Doctor's Story of Love, Loss and Consolation by Rachel Clarke (Abacus, 2020) is an incredibly soothing insight into caring for loved ones at the end of life.

For thinking about your needs as you get older, I am a great fan of the way that Dr Lucy Pollock talks about ageing in *The Book about Getting Older* (Michael Joseph, 2021) and *The Golden Rule: Lessons in Living from a Doctor of Ageing* (Michael Joseph, 2024).

I use journalist, podcaster and writer Elizabeth Day's work a lot to think about how we frame failure and disappointment: *Failosophy: A Handbook for When Things Go Wrong*, (HarperCollins, 2020) and *How to Fail: Everything I've Ever Learned from Things Going Wrong* (HarperCollins, 2019).

For tackling anxiety, I find *Rewire your Anxious Brain: How to Use the Neuroscience of Fear to End Anxiety, Panic and Worry* by Catherine M. Pittman and Elizabeth M. Karle very helpful. For new thinking around post-traumatic stress, I use *The End of Trauma: How the New Science of Resilience is Changing How We Think About PTSD* by George Bonanno (Basic Books, 2021).

Notes

1. Wrexham was granted royal status to become a city in May 2022
2. Disaster Recovery graph. This is my version of the recovery graph but with acknowledgement to Zunin, L. M., & Myers, D. (2000) where the graph was first introduced in the 'Training manual for human service workers in major disasters'. 2nd Ed. Washington, DC: Center for Mental Health Services and has been reimagined multiple times in emergency response literature.
3. The Holmes and Rahe Scale can be viewed in full here: https://www.stress.org/wp-content/uploads/2024/02/Holmes-Rahe-Stress-inventory.pdf
4. Tinson, B. (2009) *The Gresford Letters: Aftermath of a Disaster* (MiddleView)
5. Taken from the lyrics of 'Yma O Hyd', a Welsh folk song
6. Chrisafis, A., 'Mayor of Amatrice: "the town isn't here any more" after strong earthquake', *Guardian*, 24 August 2016 https://www.theguardian.com/world/2016/aug/24/strong-earthquake-hits-italy-with-people-reportedly-trapped-in-rubble
7. This work by Tracy was later dramatised in the 2020 BBC drama *The Salisbury Poisonings*

8. Taylor, A. J. W. and Frazer, A. G. (1981) 'Psychological Sequelae of Operation Overdue following the DC 10 Aircrash in Antarctica', Wellington, NZ: Victoria University
9. For more discussion on the way language is used in emergency management, see this episode of *Word of Mouth* with Michael Rosen https://www.bbc.co.uk/programmes/m001z6q1
10. See Danieli, Y. in Brenner, G., Bush, D., Moses, J. (eds) (2009) *Creating Spiritual and Psychological Resilience*, Routledge
11. Troyer, J. (2023) 'I Thought I Knew Everything about Death. Then Grief Struck Me', *Psyche*, 16 May 2023 https://psyche.co/ideas/i-thought-i-knew-everything-about-death-then-grief-struck-me
12. For Andrew's full account of this see Ecott, T., 'I felt like it was time to let go. I couldn't be bothered fighting any more', *Guardian*, 9 August 2009 https://www.theguardian.com/uk/2009/aug/09/marchioness-pleasure-boat-survivor
13. Ibid.
14. McNaughton, E., Wills, J. and Lallemant, D. (2015) *Leading in Disaster Recovery: A Companion through the Chaos*, New Zealand Red Cross leading_in_disaster_recovery_a_companion_through_the_chaos.pdf (preparecenter.org)
15. Redfern, C., 'Your life is under threat. You might have to run at any second. What do you take?' *Guardian*, 2 April 2022 https://www.theguardian.com/global-development/2022/apr/02/emergency-bags-packed-for-quick-getaway-activists-fires-floods
16. For a longer explanation see https://www.simplypsychology.org/maslow.html
17. I found this a useful essay on new thinking around Maslow: Copley, L., 'Hierarchy of Needs: A 2024 Take

on Maslow's Findings', *Positive Psychology*, 2 October 2024 https://positivepsychology.com/hierarchy-of-needs/
18. The exposure of abuse in the aid world has highlighted corruption – e.g. see https://www.independent.co.uk/news/uk/home-news/oxfam-child-abuse-haiti-scandal-inquiry-sexual-exploitation-charity-commission-a8953566.html
19. 'Independent Panel Report into Fans' Experiences at the 2022 European Champions League Final', Queen's University Belfast, 17 October 2022 https://www.qub.ac.uk/News/Allnews/2022/IndependentPanelReportintoFansExperiencesatthe2022EuropeanChampionsLeagueFinal.html
20. These cards are available from https://hummingly.co
21. For further information on this see https://www.thetimes.com/uk/healthcare/article/graseby-syringe-pumps-ditched-by-nhs-were-donated-overseas-vhgqs0z6z
22. Training of medical students with anaesthetised patients does still take place but medical school regulations now state that the patient should have consented first. For further information see https://www.gmc-uk.org/professional-standards/professional-standards-for-doctors/intimate-examinations-and-chaperones/intimate-examinations-and-chaperones
23. Kipling, Rudyard (1917) 'The Land' https://www.kiplingsociety.co.uk/poem/poems_land.htm
24. This was a term coined by musician Nick Cave in 2024, 'Nick Cave: "Hopefulness Is Not a Neutral Position – It Is Adversarial"', *Relevant Magazine*, 15 August 2024 https://relevantmagazine.com/culture/nick-cave-hopefulness-is-not-a-neutral-position-it-is-adversarial/
25. This was a term coined by cancer campaigner Deborah James after her diagnosis in 2016 https://www.hopeforall.org.uk/read/rebellious-hope/

26. See, Buckley, J., 'Professor Phil Scraton Recounts His Dogged Fight for Hillsborough Victims', *Sydney Morning Herald*, 28 October 2016 https://www.smh.com.au/sport/soccer/professor-phil-scraton-recounts-his-dogged-fight-for-hillsborough-victims-20161028-gscvl8.html
27. Reade, B. (2008) *43 Years with the Same Bird*, Macmillan Publishing, p.143
28. Newburn, T. 'Racism? Poverty, drink and social media? We still don't know why Britons rioted a month ago – and we need answers', *Guardian*, 4 September 2024 https://www.theguardian.com/commentisfree/article/2024/sep/04/riots-racism-poverty-drink-social-media-southport
29. This explanation was extracted from the work of Gerald Vizenor. See Vizenor, G. (2008) *Survivance: Narratives of Native Presence*, Lincoln, NE: University of Nebraska Press
30. *You Know you are from Christchurch when...* compiled by Bruce Raines and available from online book retailers. You can also still visit the Facebook page that compiles the jokes
31. Skaife, S. and Martyn, J. (2022) *Art Psychotherapy Groups in The Hostile Environment of Neoliberalism: Collusion or Resistance?* Routledge
32. 'Epigenetics and Child Development: How Children's Experiences Affect Their Genes', Harvard University, 19 February 2019 https://developingchild.harvard.edu/resources/infographics/what-is-epigenetics-and-how-does-it-relate-to-child-development/
33. Furuyashiki, A. et al. (2019) 'A comparative study of the physiological and psychological effects of forest bathing (*Shinrin-yoku*) on working age people with and without depressive tendencies', *Environmental Health and Preventatitve Medicine*, 24; 46 https://www.ncbi.nlm.nih.gov/pmc/articles/PMC6589172/

34. As well as mass fatalities, forensic odontology is also used in the criminal justice system for analysing evidence such as bite marks
35. 'Great Fire of London: How science rebuilt a city', Science Museum, https://www.sciencemuseum.org.uk/objects-and-stories/great-fire-london-how-science-rebuilt-city
36. Indeed the trauma of the fire and its aftermath is captured in the diaries of Samuel Pepys – Wheatley, Henry B. (ed) (1904, 1663) *The Diaries of Samuel Pepys*. vol 4. Bell and Sons
37. Ibid.
38. See Matthew Hogan's blog on the journey to memorialisation here https://mtthwhgn.com and Brataas, K. (2025) *Disaster Memorials and Monuments: History, Context and Practice from around the World*, Routledge https://www.routledge.com/Disaster-Memorials-and-Monuments-History-Context-and-Practice-from-around-the-World/Brataas/p/book/9781032523323
39. Munster, B., 'Italy's budget mess leaves earthquake-stricken towns in limbo', *Politico*, 20 August 2024 https://www.politico.eu/article/amatrice-earthquake-italy-budget-limbo/
40. Leech, C. (1981) *Letter to a Younger Son*, Weidenfeld & Nicolson

Index

absence management 39
abusive relationships 143–44
acceptance 66–69
　of truths 184–85
active listening 93
addictions 226
adolescents 111, 203–4
advice, false 145–46
advocacy groups 86
afterwards, energy of 243
afterwards, the 245–49
agency 127, 154
agenda-less meeting, the 70
agony aunts 185–86
aid, clearing up 121–22
alcohol and alcohol use 120, 218, 226
alienation 181
Alison (responder) 221
allies 89–90
allyship 38–39, 134
altruism 91–92
Amatrice earthquake, 2016 42–46
　damage 43, 44
　death toll 42–43
　fireman 43–44, 45–46
　the honeymoon phase 43
　impact assessment 43–46
　loss 47
　New Zealand woman 45–46
　rebuilding 48, 246
　the slump 46–47
　uptick 48
ambiguous loss, sense of 44–45
Amesbury, Novichok poisoning cases 52–56
Angelou, Maya 7
anger 28, 67, 87
Anne (friend) 197–98
anniversaries 38, 199, 202, 238
antenatal care 104
anxiety 9, 72, 110–11, 221, 226
anxiety audits 119–20
Ari (Track and Trace helpline caller) 207–8
Army, the 19–20
arsehole territory, descent into 222–23
art therapy 82, 242
assembly presentation 138
Australian Red Cross 84

authority, anger against 5
autonomy, loss of 128

baby booms 104
bad help ambivalence 123
bad news 251
　truthful delivery 167–69
batteries 117
behaviour analysis 225–26
behaviour changes 57
behaviour policing 203
bereaved mums, grief policing 193
bereavement 61, 62, 88, 135, 216–17
bereavement literature 104
betrayal, sense of 87–88
Bex (senior emergency planner) 10, 257
biases 163, 164
Big Cry, the 222
birth control 104
blame 47–48
　toxic 58–59
Bloody Sunday, 1972 170–71
bluntness, tempering 153
Bosnia 176, 221
boundaried care 224–25
Bowbelle (dredger) 77, 78, 90
The Braer disaster 239–40
breathwork and breathing exercises 72, 217–18
bricolage 196
Build Back Better narrative 231
burnout monitors 71, 223
Bush, Barbara 125
business impact assessment 55–56

calamity cards 112–13, 156
calmness 156
campaigners 186–87
campaigns, compartmentalisation 70–71
candles 117
care workers 216
carers, and needs 118
#CashNotStuff 138
Castaway (film) 64
castaway effect 64–66
catharsis, and laughter 194
censorship 176
Champions League final, 2022 108–9

change
  positive 149–51
  and rebuilding 246–47
charities 19–20
Chaz (dog) 216–17
child abuse 216
children 62–63, 65, 84–85, 179
  COVID 19 pandemic 214
  Grenfell fire 200–1, 204
  lost 65–66
  needs 107
  supporting 63
  survivance 200–1, 203–4
  voice 200–1, 203
Christchurch earthquake, 2011 45–46, 194
chronic emergency 147
chronic illness 49
chronic stress 178
classism 178
clearing out 234
climate change 147–49, 150
Clinton, Bill 231
clothing
  donated 122–23
  home clothes 218
  layering 117–18
  work clothes 218
cognitive behavioural therapy 220
Come from Away (musical) 123
comfort 65–66, 167
coming home 223
communities of circumstance 61
community acceptance 66–67
community exclusion 50
community groups, fragmentation of 28
community truth 169
companionable silence 212
compartmentalisation 3, 186–87
compassion 54, 131, 182
conditioning 163
conflicting narratives 171
conflicting views, emergency planning philosophy on 160
connection, need for 116, 119
consequences 113
  circle of 62
conspiracy theories 193
coping strategies 5–6, 196–97, 217–25, 225–27
  breathwork 217–18
  flashbacks 219–23
  growing plants 217
  holidays 218–19
  laughter 192–96
  long-term 226–27
  music 218
  peer support groups 197–200
  talking to yourself 223–25
  therapy 219–23, 225
  wardrobes 218
coroners 165–67
courage, in help 135–36
COVID 19 pandemic 1, 4–5, 57, 91, 132, 151–52, 177–78, 180–81, 197, 203–4, 222–23
  anxiety 110–11
  children 214
  frontline disaster responders 209
  National Covid Memorial Wall 231–33, 235
  rebuilding 246, 248
  sense of shared experience 213–14
  Track and Trace system 207–8
CPR 118
crisis, moments of 1

crisis support workers 127–28
criticism 185
crowdfunding 126
crude oil spills 239–40
cruelty, tempering 153
CUIDAR project 203
curiosity 179

Dad's souk 136–37
danger, level of 5–6
Danieli, Yael 67–68
Daszkiewicz, Tracy 54–56
daytime routine 92–93
death, inevitability of 160
Deb (aunt) 233
deception 164
decision-making 88–89, 254–55
decontamination activities 53
deep knowledge 108
Defence Chemical Biological Radiological and Nuclear Centre, Porton Down 52
defibrillators 118
denial 64, 65–66
depression 119
dialogue 146
diary, planning 38
difficult conversations 112
dignity 136–37, 247
  importance of 129–32
  use of term 130
direct action 202
directors of public health 54
disappointments, letting go of 71–72
disaster
  author's experience of 1–2
  conceptualisation 12
  heuristics 13
Disaster Action 198–99
disaster aftermath, stages 20–21
disaster classification 60
disaster go bag 116–18
disaster identification work 214–15
disaster path 19–20
disaster patinas 235–36
disaster pollution 122
disaster recovery, applicability 110
disaster recovery graph 19–23, 20–21, 40
  author's role 21–23
  emotional highs and lows 20–21
  euphoria 26–27, 33–34
  gift of 36–7
  importance 23, 30
  incubation phase 23–25
  introducing 33
  magic of 35
  the moment of impact 25–26
  pendulum swings 30
  recovery phase 30
  the slump 28–29, 34–35, 37
  as support 37
  survivance 29–30
  time taken 37
  universality 23
  uptick 29–30, 36–37
  utility 21
disaster responders 19–20
  emotional danger 33
  guidance document 84
  humour 194
disaster response training 32–33
disasters, unequal impacts 55

Index

discomfort 43–44
disillusionment 28
distress 28
 unresolved 29
divisions 86–87
Dix, Pam 104–5
domestic violence 216
donated items
 assembly presentation 138
 clearing up 121–22
 clothing 122–23
 money 138
 receiving 123
doom-mongering 149
door keys 100
dreams 77, 79

earthquakes
 aftershocks 45–46
 Amatrice, Italy, 2016 42–46
 Christchurch, 2011 45–46, 194
 damage 43, 44
Easthope, Lucy
 baby losses 51
 bike stabilisers 8
 childhood 75–76
 coping strategies 5–6, 196–97, 217–25
 COVID 19 pandemic 4
 daughters 146, 163
 death of Chaz 216–17
 death of father 10–12, 64, 102, 135, 253–54
 defiance 201–2
 emergency planner role 21–23
 enthusiasm 219
 experience of disaster 1–2
 father's funeral 196
 first call 156
 first dead man 8
 grandmother 254–56
 husband's atypical Ménière's disease diagnosis 196–97, 243–45
 influence of father 7–8, 256–57
 internship 170–72
 Jersey disaster response training 32–33
 kidney infections 129–30
 memorialisation of father 233–34
 mentors 219
 as a mother 9–10
 mother 102
 pride in scars 210
 relationship with hope 142–43
 relationship with husband 210–12
 and risk 8–9
 slump 86
Easthope, Tom 196–97, 210–12, 243–45, 250
Elizabeth (colleague) 112, 156
Elizabeth II, Queen, Regal slight story 169, 181
embarrassment 133
emergency planners 1–2, 9, 21–22
 approach 64
 burden 24–25
 and home lives 10
 impact 3
 unheeded work 3
 veteran stories 13
emergency planning philosophy 160
emergency plans 23
emergency preparedness 116–18
emergency services 19–20
emotional danger 33
emotional highs and lows, mapping 20–21

emotional labour 85–86, 196
emotional trauma 214–15
empaths 221
end-of-life care 153
energy, of afterwards 243
enthusiasm 137
Eric (dentist) 214–15
esteem and self-actualisation, need for 105–6
ethical framework 249
euphoria 26–27
evacuation planning 159
events, versions of 163–65
expectation, pressure of 58
extreme weather events 148
eye movement desensitisation and reprogramming (EMDR) 109

facilitation, external 70
fact checking 170
facts, confronting 66–67
failures, letting go of 71–72
Fairbourne 147–48
fall-outs 84
false advice 145–46
false hope 65–66
families' rights 55
family 57
family crises 182
family relationships, strain on 86
far right groups 177–79
fears, framing 22
feedback 185
fire damp 16
fire services 50
fixity, harms 67
flashbacks 79, 210–17
 coping strategies 219–23, 225–27
 inducers 218
flexibility 251
flight, things taken 95–96
flooding
 bad help 121–22
 and climate change 147–48
 rebuilding 191–92
 secondary 41
flowers, care for 22
food 91, 112, 116, 138
forensic dentistry 215–16
forensic odontology 215–16
forensic uncertainty 28
forest bathing 205–6
forward motion 234–35
Foulkes, Lucy 111
fraud 159
Frazer, A. 60
friendships 48–49, 87, 183, 199
fun, building 206
funeral directors 93
funeral talk 134
FUN-erals 196
future, the, looking towards 241–43

general practitioners 35–36
Generation Z 169
genocide 176
genocide survivors 67–68
gentle help 258
geopolitical tensions 6
ghoulish sightseers 104–5
Giuliani, Rudy 140
Glancy, Diane 190

government, hunger for data 41
governments, bad help 124–25
Grand Vaux region, flooding, 2023 31
gratitude 234–35
Great Epiphany, the 241–43, 243–45, 250–51
Great Exodus, the 241, 243, 243–45, 250–51
Great Fire of London 229–30, 245–46, 246
green shoots 92
Grenfell day 189
Grenfell fire, 2017 61, 65–66, 80–83, 90, 123, 202
 children 200–201, 204
 deaths 81
 incubation phase 81
 inquiry report 82
 lack of honeymoon 81–82
 support 83–86
Gresford mine disaster 15–17, 36–37, 144
 casualties 16
 commemoration 18
 explosion 17
 honeymoon phase 26–27
 incubation phase 23
 legacy 17–19
 memorialisation 238–39
 pre-event 16–17
 rebuilding 246
 the slump 28
 uptick 29
grief 11, 27, 68–69, 86
 denial phase 64, 65, 66
 magical thinking 102
 policing 193
grief counselling 68
Griffiths, Paul and Elaine 249
grounding 205
grudges 92
Guardian 96
guidance document 84
guilt, toxic 58–59

hair stylists 216
harms
 counting 72–73
 finding 56–59
 fixity 67
 of help 130–31
 intangible 51–59
 tangible 53
 unseeable 54
healing 225–26
 barriers to 73
health checks 91
health scandal, 2018 124
heard, need to be 114
heartsickness 47–48
hedonic adaptation 119
Helen (responder) 221
help
 asking for 133
 backing off 136
 bad 121–32
 bingo card of bad help 126–28
 British approach 125
 colonial legacy 125
 courage in 135–36
 crowdfunding 126
 and dignity 129–32, 136–37
 enlisting 71
 food 138
 good 128, 132–37

and gratitude 125–26
harm of 130–31
intentional 137–38
listening 132–33
malevolent offloading of crap 124
misdirected 122
motivations behind 125
non-verbal 134
offering 133
overpromising 27, 126, 137–38
pay forward 133–34
performative 128
and prejudice 125
tiny 136
toxic positivity 127
understanding 132–34
helplessness 5
Henry Dickens Community Centre 189, 195, 202, 204, 242
hero narratives 58
Hett, Martyn 102–3
heuristics 13
hidden impacts 56
hidden needs 101, 103–4
hidden victims 59–61
hierarchy, imagined 79
Hilbre Islands 75–76, 89
Hillsborough disaster, 1989 108, 172–75
Hillsborough Independent Panel Report 174, 175
hindsight 174
hiraeth 47–49
historical disasters 229–30
holidays 218–19
Holmes and Rahe scale of stressful life events 26
Holocaust survivors 67–68
home clothes 218
honesty 152
honeymoon phase, the 26–27, 33, 43
hope 139–40, 142–43, 154–58
 difference from hopium 143–44, 151–54
 growth of 157
 holding onto 158
 importance of 145–46
 manifest 158–59
 and positive changes 149–51
 as strength 160–61
 warrior emotion 158
hopium 140, 142–45, 152–54
 blight of 150
 and climate change 147–49
 conceptualisation 142
 danger of 142, 144
 and denial 152–54
 difference from hope 143–44, 151–54
 false advice 145–46
 organisational role in 144–45
 wariness of 154–55
hospices 32, 103
hospital bags 118
household incidents 24–25
human consequences 20
human rights abuses 176
humour 192–96, 198
Hurricane Betsy, 1965 141
Hurricane Katrina, 2005 125, 139–42
 damage 141–42
 death toll 139, 141
 human failures 140–41
 power 140
 Women of the Storm group 195
Hurricane Mitch, 1998 122

Index

hurt 87–88
identification work 214–15
imagery 6–7, 115, 216–17
imagination 216–17
impact, moment of 25–26
impact assessment 42, 49–51
  Amatrice earthquake, 2016 43–46
  business 55–56
  content 49
  difficulty 50
  first stage 69
  forgotten demographics 59–60
  hidden impacts 56
  human side 45–46
  intangible harms 51–56
  list of harms 50–51
  militaristic 53
  Novichok poisoning cases 53–56
  psychological impacts 58–59
  ripple effects 59–63
  role 49
  setbacks 63
  taking stock 66–69
  toxic positivity 51
  value of 63
impossible needs 101, 102
incubation phase 23–25
indescribable loss, describing 47
Indian Ocean tsunami, 2004 99–101, 231
  bad help 124
  as totem of the future 84–85
Indigenous Americans 190–91
information sources 5–6, 159–60
inner voice 223–25
  critical 72
inquests, delay 88
inquiries 13
instinct 23–25
intangible harms 51–59
intangible needs 101, 101–2
interest, showing 37
intergenerational trauma 61–62, 108
internet 193
intimacy, need for 103–4
intolerance 68
intuition 23–25, 38
investigative research 170–72
isomorphic learning 186
Issam (human rights activist) 96
Italy, Amatrice earthquake, 2016 42–46

Jan (from Track and Trace helpline) 207–8, 223–24
Jelena (friend) 197–98
Jersey, States of
  multiple disasters 31–35
  rebuilding 246
John (friend) 68–69
Johnson, Boris 214
joie de vivre 199
joke-telling 194
Jolie (colleague) 112, 156
Jones, Katy 170–72, 183
judgement making 104–5

key workers 127–28
kintsugi 210, 225
Kipling, Rudyard, 'The Land' 137

lasagne phase, the 27
last responders 2

Latimer Community Art Therapy 84–85
laughter 192–96, 198
Leanne (friend and colleague) 48
learning 13
  isomorphic 186
L'Ecume II, sinking of 31
lessons, conceptualisation 12–13
lies 164, 168, 171
  calling out 175
life
  key lesson 212–13
  rebuilding 79–80
life before, loss of 47–49
life changes, speed of 13–14
life events, scale of stress 26
limbo 88–89
limits 158–59
listening 132–33, 183, 207–9
Lockerbie air disaster, 1988 90, 104–5
locksmiths 100
loss
  describing 47
  of the life before 47–49
Lucy, Gran 254–56
Lyubomirsky, Sonja 119

McElhenney, Rob 17
magical thinking 102
managed retreat 148, 149
Manchester Arena bombing, 2017 102–3
Manchester Monastery 248–49
Mansfield, Michael 55
Marchioness sinking, 1989 77–80
Marine Accident Investigation Board 78
Mark (responder) 221
marriage breakdowns 49
Martyn's Law 102–3
masculinity 109
Maslow, Abraham 98
media requests 199
meeting spaces 105–6
memorials and memorialisation 231–40, 249
memory 164, 165, 211, 224
menopausal symptoms 91
mental anguish, underplaying 79
mental health 58–59, 91, 109, 111, 241
mentors 219
Meredith (responder) 221
messiness 192
Mike (friend) 157–58
Mike (uncle) 165–66
mind maps 70
mining 15–17
miracles 147
misinformation 180
moment of impact 25–26
mortality, sense of 49
Mother-Earth initiated events 141
mourning 49
mud 75–76, 89
multigenerational slump 28
multiple disasters 31–35
Murray, Figen 102–3
music 197, 200–1, 202, 205, 218

naming, strength from 61–62
narrative verdict 182
narratives, forming 49
Nathan (responder) 221
National Covid Memorial Wall 231–33, 235
National Emergencies Trust 138

National Health Service 220
natural disasters 141
natural world, the 217
nature, and crude oil spills 239–40
nature-bathing 205–6
near misses 24
Nedergaard, Maiken 92–93
needful things 101–6
need-meeting 100
needs
    to be heard 114
    carers and 118
    categories 101
    connection 116, 119
    crisis of unmet 107–9
    esteem and self-actualisation 105–7
    failure to meet 106
    the feels 112, 114
    fulfilling 115
    hidden 101, 103–4
    hierarchy of 97–98, 99–101
    identification 111–16
    impossible 101, 102–3
    intangible 101, 101–2
    intimacy 103–4
    judgement making 104–5
    letting go 116
    mapping 106
    meeting 105–6
    pleasure 118–19
    practical 112, 113–14
    reframing 114–15
    responding to 112
    as rights 105, 115–16
    tangible 101
    thinking about 99
negative comparisons 251–52
new beginnings 4
New Orleans, Hurricane Katrina, 2005 125, 139–42
    damage 141–42
    death toll 139, 141
    human failures 140–41
    Women of the Storm group 195
New Zealand, Christchurch earthquake, 2011 45–46, 194
New Zealand Red Cross 84
newborns, deceased 65–66
Newburn, Tim 179
news consumption 251
news cycle 157
nihilism 150
9/11 terrorist attacks 65, 241
    memorials 236–37
no, saying 160
non-verbal help 134
Novichok poisoning cases, Salisbury 51–56

objectivity 146
olfactory trauma 218
One Truth, the 172–75, 180–82
ongoing work 190
online networks 200
optimism 143
order, imposing 26
otters 239–40
overpromising 27, 126, 137–38
overreacting 160
over-thinkers 221
overwhelm, managing 120
own things, access to 100

ownership 137
oxytocin 26, 104

pacing 135
pain
    compartmentalisation 3
    turned inwards 59
partnership breakdowns 49
past experiences, unresolved 108–9, 110–11
past quilts 109
past traumas, acknowledging 108–9
patience, survivors' lack of 45–46
paying forward 133–34
Payne, Bob 7–8, 133–34, 136–37, 231, 256–57, 258
    death 10–12, 64, 102, 135, 253–54
    funeral 196
    memorialisation 233–34
peer support groups 196–200
people-pleasing 160
people's voice, hearing 25
perfection, definition 191
permacrisis 6–7, 257
personal disaster, route through 10–12
personal effects management 33, 131–32
    censorship 131–32
    importance of 134
    returning effects 134
pet emergency plan 159
pets, loss of 62, 216–17
phantoms 210–17
pinballing 106, 115–16
planning 7, 10
    diary 38
    impact assessment 42
    slump 92
pleasure, importance of 118–19
pogroms, 2024 177–80
police 50
    welfare visits 208
Port of London Authority 78
positive changes 149–51
positivity, toxic 51, 127
post-disaster emigration 48
post-traumatic growth 202
powerlessness, feeling of 5
practical help 97
pragmatism 145, 150
precarity 257
pre-conceptions 181
pre-event, the 16–17, 23–25
prejudice 125
premonitions 24
pride 133
    in wounds 210
primary care doctors 35–36
Pritchard, Colin 166–67
problems, and unmet needs 107–9
professional community 3
proof, standard of 167
pro-social 151
protective automation 99
psychological glottal block 67
psychological harms 49
psychological impacts 58–59
public health teams 109

quiet time, value of 72

racism 178
Reade, Brian 175

Index

reading 5–6, 157
realism 145, 152
reality, facing up to 64–66
reasonable adjustments 115
Reasonable Worst-Case Scenario 149–50, 155–56
reassurance 57
rebellion, survivance 200–203
rebuilding 48, 191, 245–49
  Build Back Better narrative 231
  and change 246–47
  the Great Epiphany 241–43, 243–45, 250–51
  historical disasters 229–30
  priorities 230
reconciliation, and truth 175–76
recovery 84–85, 189–90, 202
  aspects 53
  guidance document 84
  slowness of 48
  training 191–92
recovery groups 53
recovery kit 38–39
recovery phase 20, 30, 37
regeneration 30
regret 49
relapses 204–5
remembering 221
reminders 134
reproductive medicine 104
resilience 100, 113, 143
rest 91, 112
reviews 30
Reynolds, Ryan 17
riots, 2024 177–80
risk and risk awareness 5–6
  author and 8–9
  spread of 6–7
risk management literature 54
routines 250
Rowley, Charlie, Novichok poisoning 52–56
Royal College of General Practitioners 35–36
Royal National Lifeboat Institution 76
RSPCA 159
Rudnik, Susan 82–83, 84, 90, 123
Rwandan genocide 80, 176

sadmin 88
safety, sense of 58
St Helier, gas explosion, 2022 31
Salisbury, Novichok poisoning cases 51–56
Save the Children 43, 203
savouring 256
scams and scamming 159
scene management 33
Science Museum, London 230
Scraton, Phil 172–75, 183
second opinions 38
Second World War 51, 58, 98, 255–56
secondary flooding 41
self-actualisation, need for 105–6
self-determination 123, 130–32
  right to 130
sense-checking 110–11
sense-making 59, 220–21
separation, trauma of 88
setbacks 204–5
  impact assessment 63
sexism 178
shared experience, sense of 213–14
shell shock 58
shock 64
sightseers 104–5

Skripal, Sergei, Novichok poisoning 51–56
Skripal, Yulia, Novichok poisoning 51–56
sleep 92–93, 226
slippers, accident rate linked to 25
slump, the 28–29, 34–35, 37, 46–47
  cherish green shoots 92
  depersonalising 83
  depth of 80–81
  discomfort 92
  emotional labour 85–86
  getting out of 79–80, 89–92, 235
  health check 91
  limbo of 88–89
  living inside 82–83
  necessity of 85
  pain of 86–88
  physical manifestations 81, 87
  planning 92
  processing 87
  purpose 76
  recognising 90–91
  recovery kit 92–93
  survivors' experience 77–80
  symptoms 76
  taking stock 91
smells 218
Smithsonian Museum 190–91
social media 6–7, 25, 38–39, 159–60, 170
Solnit, Rebecca 154
sorrow, codifying 26
Southport, stabbings, 2024 177–79
spiral, the 69–70
spiritual moments 35
spring cleaning 234
state-of-the-world depression 150
state-sanctioned narratives 172, 174–75
stoicism, British 51
Stormzy 202
struggle 35, 83–86
Sturgess, Dawn, Novichok poisoning 52–56
Sue (friend) 157–58
suicides 166–67, 191
support
  disaster recovery graph as 37
  outpouring of 26–27
support bubble 117
support groups 225
survivance 29–30, 189–92
  children 200–1, 203–4
  definition 190
  humour 192–96, 198
  online networks 200
  peer support groups 197–200
  rebellion 200–3
  support 196–200
survivors
  aberrance 201
  direct action 202
  discomfort 43–44
  lack of patience 45–46
  slump experience 77–80
Sutton, Andrew 77–80, 88, 90
swimming 221–22
sympathetic platitudes 167–68

taking stock 66–69, 70, 71–72, 72–73, 91
talking 146
  importance of 69
  to yourself 223–25
tangible harms 53
tangible needs 101

tattoos 237–38
Taylor, A. 60
teaching hospitals 129–30
teeth 214–15
temporality 178
tensions 84
  managing 199
Thames River Police 78
thank you, saying 234–35, 249–50
therapeutic relationships 220
therapy 102–3, 219–23, 225
time, buying 185
time limits, awareness of 258
timing 135
today, importance of 258
Toll Bar, Doncaster 143–44, 145–46, 195
tomorrow, no guarantee of 258
torches 117
total safety, assurances of 54
touch 212
toxic guilt 58–59
toxic nuggets 168
toxic positivity 51, 127
Toxteth riots, 1981 7–8
training 31, 191–92
training documents 20
trauma
  acknowledging past 108–9
  approaches to 90
  exposure to 212–17
  and listening 209
  triggers 109
trauma therapy 109
trauma-worms 216
triage 3
trivial things, intolerance of 68
trust, loss of 144–45
truth
  burying 176
  catharsis of 175
  censorship 176
  the One Truth 172–75, 180–82
  and reconciliation 175–76
  struggle for 174
  uncomfortable 180
truths
  accepting 184–85
  balancing 165–67
  and breaking bad news 167–69
  burden of 184
  and coercion 182
  compartmentalisation 186–87
  compromise 171–72
  conflict between 169, 180–82
  contradiction 171
  distillation to one narrative 167
  enquire 185
  forcing an agreement 175–76
  holding multiple 182–84
  inconsistencies 165–66
  interregnum period of 176–77
  investigative research 170–72
  juggling 165–66, 179–80
  listening to 183

mining for 170–72
multiple 169, 171, 179
narrative verdict 182
navigating 182, 186
the One Truth 172–75, 180–82
Regal slight story 169, 181
stance-taking 180–82
state-sanctioned narratives 172, 174–75
  and trust 167–68
universal themes 186
versions of 163–65
TV researchers 27
Typhoon Haiyan, 2013 124–25

uncertainty 14, 150, 258
unexploded bombs 96–97
United States of America 140
unmet needs, crisis of 107–9
unprecedented, tendency to use term 19
unseeable harms 54
US Federal Emergency Management Agency Higher
    Education conference 190

vigils 192
virtual reality technology 65
voice
  calm 156
  children 200–1, 203
  inner 223–25
  people's 25
vulnerability, sense of 49

war imagery 6
Welcome to Wrexham (TV series) 17, 18–19, 28, 29
welfare visits 208
wellbeing 208–9
wellbeing training 224–25
what comes next, articulating 46
whatever next attitude 256–57
white lies 168
wider community, the 61
widow grief 135
widow's fire 104
The Wirral 75–76, 89
The Wirral Globe 76
wishful thinking 151
Women of the Storm group 195
wonder, sense of 256
work clothes 218
World Trade Center, 9/11 terrorist attacks 65
worry 9, 107
worst-case scenario thinking 155–56, 158
wounds
  exposure to trauma 212–17
  flashbacks 210–17
  pride in 210
  repairing 210
Wrexham, Gresford mine disaster 15–19, 23, 26–27,
    28, 29, 36–37, 238, 246
Wrexham Leader 18
writing 70
www.bacp.co.uk 225

Yorkshire flooding 121–22